GET THE PICTURE

VISUAL LITERACY
in Content-Area Instruction

Marva Cappello, Ph.D., and Nancy T. Walker, Ph.D.

Foreword by Diane Lapp, Ed.D.

Publishing Credits

Corinne Burton, M.A.Ed., *Publisher*
Conni Medina, M.A.Ed., *Editor in Chief*
Nika Fabienke, Ed.D., *Content Director*
Véronique Bos, *Creative Director*
James Anderson, M.S.Ed., *Director of EdTech*
Shaun Bernadou, *Art Director*

Susan Daddis, M.A.Ed, *Editor*
John Leach, *Assistant Editor*
Jessica Tran, *EdTech Specialist*
Regina Frank, *Graphic Designer*
Walter Mladina, *Photo Editor*

Image Credits

p.33, p.41, p.104, p.172 Bettmann/Getty Images; p.35 Louvre Museum; p.174, p.189 (top left) The Metropolitan Museum of Art; p.178 Library of Congress [LC-USZC4-6445]; p.180 Library of Congress [LC-USZ62-136123]; p.184 Library of Congress [LC-DIG-nclc-03225]; p.188 (top left) Musée d'Orsay; p.188 (top right) The National Gallery UK; p.188 (bottom right) Private collection via Christie's; p.188 (bottom left) Philadelphia Museum of Art; p.189 (top right) Indianapolis Museum of Art; p.189 (bottom right) Österreichische Galerie Belvedere; p.189 (bottom left) Van Gogh Museum, Netherlands; p.192 Andres Ryoma; p.198 (bottom left) Private collection via Sotheby's; all other images from iStock and/or Shutterstock.

Standards

© 2014 Mid-continent Research for Education and Learning (McREL)
TEKS © Copyright 2018 Texas Education Association (TEA). All rights reserved.
© 2010 National Council for the Social Studies (NCSS), The College, Career, and Civic Life (C3) Framework for Social Studies State Standards: Guidance for Enhancing the Rigor of K–12 Civics, Economics, Geography, and History.
© Copyright 2010. National Governors Association Center for Best Practices and Council of Chief State School Officers. All rights reserved.
ISTE Standards for Students, ©2016, ISTE® (International Society for Technology in Education), iste.org. All rights reserved.
© 2014 Mid-continent Research for Education and Learning
Copyright © 2010 National Council for the Social Studies
NGSS Lead States. 2013. Next Generation Science Standards: For States, By States. Washington, DC: The National Academies Press.
© Copyright 2007–2018 Texas Education Agency (TEA). All rights reserved.
© 2007 Teachers of English to Speakers of Other Languages, Inc. (TESOL)
© 2014 Board of Regents of the University of Wisconsin System, on behalf of WIDA— www.wida.us.

Shell Education

5301 Oceanus Drive
Huntington Beach, CA 92649-1030
www.tcmpub.com/shell-education
ISBN 978-1-4938-8080-5
©2020 Shell Education Publishing, Inc

Table of Contents

Foreword

Just about every month, one of the journals I read addresses the importance of developing students' visual-literacy skills. The premise is often that "learning is enhanced through multichannel processing...because we have an amazing capacity for visual memory, written or spoken information paired with visual information results in better recall" (Cozolino 2013, 232–233).

Realizing this, educators write curriculum and design instruction that captures the excitement and enthusiasm shown by students in their social media communications shared as memes, posts on Instagram, and GIFs. Additionally, watching students read and write on smartphones has caused teachers to stop demanding that phones be tucked away and instead they are asking, "How can I use students' excitement about visual messaging to promote literacy instruction?"

Teachers are also noticing that students can attend to social communication for great lengths of time, reflect on the message, and make a quick response. Although they see students paying attention to what they are viewing, what they are hearing, what they are reading, and what they are crafting as responses, teachers wonder, "Are they just being visual consumers, or are they critical reflectors of the messages they are receiving and sending?"

To be a critical communicator, it is essential that one know the importance of evaluating the veracity of a shared message and how to do so. Being able to analyze a shared message and its intended effect is the earmark of being critically literate. It is this ability to critically analyze information that teachers across the grades and disciplines strive to promote through their instruction. They ensure the development of this awareness by incorporating both the production and consumption of visual media into their instruction and into assignments. Teachers designing visual-literacy instruction may ask an array of questions:

- **What is visual literacy?**
- **What criteria should be used to select a visual text?**
- **What does a visual literacy lesson look like in the primary grades?**
- **What types of assignments promote students' engagement and evaluation of visual literacy?**
- **How can I incorporate visual texts into my instruction?**

Fortunately, the authors of *Visual Literacy in Content-Area Instruction* anticipated these and related questions. They have shared such instructionally significant information that any teacher reading their text will feel supported in extending his or her literacy curriculum to include a focus on visual texts. We are surrounded by visuals, and authors Marva Cappello and Nancy Walker help us understand how to teach students to "read," analyze, and create them. They have included instructional ideas to support and differentiate instruction for all students including English learners.

So, wait no longer to get started with Visual Literacy Instruction because you now have a guide to support you. Even if you are not a digital native, you are a visual native, and knowing this is your first step in understanding the power that visuals have in literacy learning and literacy instruction.

– Diane Lapp, Ed.D.

Distinguished Professor of Education, San Diego State University
Instructional Coach and Teacher, Health Sciences High and Middle College

Acknowledgments

Many thanks to Monica Castillo, an insightful administrator and former student who believes visual texts and visual thinking should be a valued component in the literacy curriculum. She welcomed me into two different schools in Chula Vista, California, to try on, practice, and refine many of the strategies in this text. Classroom teachers, also former students, opened their doors and their minds to the potential of these strategies. Thank you, Krista Cartier, Lisa Zapolski, Jackie Evangelou, Sheila Carreon, and Jennifer Matlock as well as Julia Gefell.

Great appreciation goes to my behind-the-scenes editor and favorite screenwriter, Nile Cappello, who lives a writer's life every day.

Both Nancy and I want to thank our colleagues Sara Johnson and Conni Medina, who first believed in this project, and Nika Fabienke, content director, who helped us across the finish line.

— **Marva Cappello, Ph.D.**

Much appreciation to Nancy Sherod, who was eager to capitalize on an opportunity to empower all students in their learning. Nancy introduced me to several elementary schools in Upland, California, that embraced and enhanced the visual-based strategies that I demonstrated. Thank you, Wendy Williamson, Xochitl Grothe-Kearns, Julie Phillips, and Cindy Steuben. Additional thanks to Tanya Reader for her insights as well.

I am forever grateful to Michael T. Roberts for his unwavering support and enthusiasm throughout this project.

— **Nancy T. Walker, Ph.D.**

Teaching Visual Texts

Every day, we are faced with thousands of images as we navigate our lives out of school. We are bombarded with a high volume of images, but that does not imply we know how to make sense of the visual texts that come our way. Many of us can navigate a map, follow steps in a diagram, or comprehend information on a billboard. In addition, digital texts almost always include visuals, and many of our students are masters at visual-based social media, including locating and creating memes to express emotion and information in efficient ways. But most of us interact passively with the powerfully visual messages, without focused attention. In a world where students' interactions with visual texts continue to grow, they will need new skills and strategies to bring to experiences (Serafini 2012).

Communication has shifted from reading words on a page to navigating a wide range of text sources in a world that is overwhelmingly visual in nature. Now, being literate must include the ability to analyze and create through visual communication. Messages are perceived to be incomplete without visuals, and therefore, we must expand our definitions of literacy and what it means to be literate. Literacy learning is no longer limited to reading, writing, listening, and speaking; we must include visual communication.

Literacy researchers have long acknowledged the role of visuals in the language arts. The *Standards for the Language Arts*, jointly published by the International Reading Association and National Council of Teachers of English in 1996, refer to

Visual Communication

Reading   Writing   Viewing   Responding

the language arts as reading, writing, listening, speaking, viewing, and visually representing. However, little attention has been paid to the roles of viewing and visually representing ideas as literacy. More recently, the College and Career Readiness (CCR) Standards added support for enlarging our definitions of literacy to include visual texts. The Common Core State Standards for English Language Arts & Literacy in History/Social Studies, Science, and Technical Subjects require students to create and analyze an "extensive range of print and nonprint texts in media forms old and new" (NGACBP and CCSSO 2010, 4). The CCR Standards also require additional focus on information texts within the disciplines that regularly utilize visual texts to communicate complex content understanding. Thus, "inherent in the Common Core State Standards is the push to help students develop the ability to interpret and communicate information visually" (Castek and Beach 2013, 556). In the new Texas Essential Knowledge and Skills adopted for the 2019 school year, students are expected to "respond to an increasingly challenging variety of sources that are read, heard, or viewed" (SBOE 2019, §110.4[b][7]) They can respond using writing, graphic organizers, illustrations, or other products. Visual texts have long been evident in our content-area textbooks, published rich with maps, graphs, charts, photographs, and other visual resources. This book will help teachers make sense of those assets for instruction.

TERMS TO KNOW

multimodal

texts that use multiple modes or communication systems to express ideas and information

Each mode expresses meanings in different ways. In this text, we focus on textual modes (including written language) and visual modes (such as drawings and photography), both on how we use them to communicate and on the ways they work together in texts.

"[When using visual text,] students who are not always as successful with text seemed to feel on equal ground with their more academically successful peers because they can all see, so no one had the upper hand."—Roper, classroom teacher

The expectation to include more visuals in the classroom has implications for our instruction. It should shift the way we think about literacy and the language arts, just as text has shifted from words on a flat surface to multidimensional and multimodal messages.

We highlight two different and important approaches to using images in your instructional practice. We provide strategies for viewing images (reading) to access and understand curriculum. We also offer ways for students to visually represent (illustrate) ideas that communicate and demonstrate understanding. Within these two approaches, we share instructional ideas where the visual texts become scaffolds for more traditional literacy goals in reading and writing.

This book is written for teachers who are ready to capitalize on the visual nature of our students' worlds outside of school to enhance and transform their instruction. But first, let's be clear about what we mean when we talk about visual texts.

What Are Visual Texts?

Throughout this book, the term *visual texts* is used to represent the general products viewed and created as part of the strategies. Visual texts are expressions that use pictorial features to communicate understanding and make meaning. While many terms more specifically describe individual types of images, this broad term represents all the pictorials used for instruction, including drawings, photographs, illustrations, icons, graphic organizers, painting, infographics, maps, charts, and memes to name but a few. Referring to visuals as *texts* is also important for educators to understand these resources as valued instructional materials.

Each of these visual texts comes with its own purposes and benefits, a few of which are illustrated in the chart. This wide range of examples represents both traditional and more modern modes of pictorial communication. Visual texts are found in sanctioned textbooks, Creative Commons, museum stores, and archive websites as well as many other sources. Teachers need to choose appropriate texts to meet instructional goals. Section 2 discusses considerations for choosing visual texts and provides support for teachers making decisions about their instructional practice.

TERMS TO KNOW

visual texts

an umbrella term for all pictorials used in instruction

Representations of Visual Texts

Photo   Painting   Drawing

Cartoon   Chart   Emoji   Advertisement

Benefits to Visual-Based Instruction

The research literature and teachers' voices both validate the many benefits to using visual-based strategies to support literacy across the curriculum. These advantages help "even the playing field" (Holloway 2012, 10) for the students in classrooms who may be new to English or face other academic challenges. The use of visual-based literacy strategies has many assets, including the following:

- **multiple ways to access curriculum**
- **expanding thinking**
- **metacognitive awareness**
- **academic vocabulary development**
- **accountable talk**
- **student engagement**
- **risk taking**

Taking all these advantages together, visual-based strategies can serve as equitable instructional practice.

Multiple Ways to Access the Curriculum

As discussed, representation of meaning occurs through multiple communication modes. Indeed, "different modes have different potential for expressing meaning" (Albers 2006, 77). When choosing instructional methods for literacy, teachers must consider what the content dictates as well as students' needs. Different communication modes are best suited to express different content understandings, and some better serve varying student learning styles.

In some cases, visuals are simply more effective at conveying meaning. For example, an author may write several paragraphs describing family relationships. The text in Figure 1.1 accurately describes the relationships. However, it is difficult to keep track of the connections because there are many characters mentioned, and it becomes confusing. The same information (plus expanded relationships) can be much more clearly and effectively communicated through a family tree as in Figure 1.2. In this case, visuals are the preferred literacy method for communicating ideas.

In addition, students need multiple routes toward understanding. Sound instructional practice provides a variety of approaches. Some students will best engage with information through the written word. Others will benefit from oral instruction, and still others will thrive using visual communication tools. Since visual learners focus best when they can see information, why not capitalize on their preferred learning style? Here, a student describes how she felt while working with visual texts in the classroom.

"The visual thinking helped me the most because first you look at the picture and wonder what's going to happen. It's curiosity."—**student using visual texts**

My grandparents, aunts, uncles, cousins, and second
cousins on my mother's side are all related to the
Romanov family. My mother is a descendant of Ivan VI.
He lived in Russia a long time ago. Ivan came from a
long line of rulers. He was the Emperor of Russia in the
18th century. My mother's family came to the U.S. from
Russia, which means that I am Russian too.

Figure 1.1 example of descriptive writing

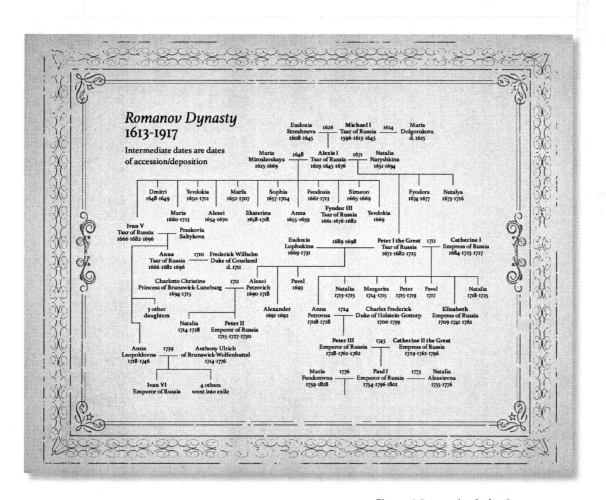

Figure 1.2 example of a family tree

Furthermore, there is evidence that visual thinking precedes traditional school literacy knowledge (Sinatra 1986). Children know that a pictogram of a man or woman indicates a restroom before they can read the words *men* or *women*. They easily manipulate icons on touch screens, interpreting their meaning often before they can explain it in words. Today's world is a visual world, yet the role that images can play in engaging and supporting our students is not always acknowledged.

Expanded Thinking

Another benefit of using visual texts is that they expand and deepen students' thinking about content. This is the ticket to comprehension. Over 20 years of research show that experience with visual media "is not just a route to better visual comprehension but also may lead to a general enhancement of cognitive abilities" (Messaris 1994, 3). Indeed, visuals "enhance [students'] thinking and help them become better readers, writers, and thinkers" (Albers 2001, 9).

Teachers advocate for visual-based strategies to help students validate their ideas. Students find supporting evidence in visual texts to justify their claims (Cappello and Lafferty 2015; Cappello and Walker 2016). Further, students learn to use appropriate language, including *because, for example*, and *the picture shows* to validate their assertions.

1.
I think that the kids are going to sail somewhere just that they are going to use magic. And also I see a castle.

2.
What is going on is probably that they are moving because they have back packs and suitcases. They are probably a family because I see that there is a mom and a dad.

two student examples of working with visual texts

Researchers have found that students expand and deepen thinking as they demonstrate their problem-solving and reasoning skills (Britsch 2009; Heath and Wolf 2005). In other cases, visuals helped students retain information (Gangwer 2005) and create deep memories (Kandel 2012), leading to enhanced comprehension. Furthermore, for emergent bilingual students, visuals can "provide a bridge from conversational to academic interaction" (Britsch 2010, 173). This has important consequences for our diverse student populations. One English learner felt "good" about using visuals "because I'm more talking ingles [sic] for your class!"

Metacognitive Awareness

Teachers want students to monitor their thinking as they participate in instruction. The use of visual texts provides students with opportunities to enhance their ability to reflect and use other metacognitive skills. Flavell defines metacognition as the monitoring of one's own "memory, comprehension, and other cognitive enterprises" (1977, 906). This ability plays an important role in problem solving, self-learning, attention, and memory.

metacognition

the awareness of one's own cognitive processes that creates self-regulated learning

It is important for teachers to nurture the belief that their students can capably interact with complex text, complicated ideas, and challenging problems across the disciplines. Research shows that visual imagery helps students monitor their comprehension during reading (Gambrell and Jawitz 1993; Wilhelm 1997). Experiences with visual texts may enhance student learning and reflection because they help students see what they know (Cappello and Lafferty 2015). Indeed, visual texts can create experiences where students reflect on their learning and question their understanding. In addition, using visual texts for reflection has been shown to have essential benefits for English learners. Cortazzi and Jin "found that using visual support and visual means of modeling stories is a crucial component to developing oral narrative skills, which in turn helps to develop [emergent bilingual] children's metacognitive and written skills" (2007, 654). These engagements allow students to self-regulate their learning, which is important for metacognition to occur (Flavell 1977).

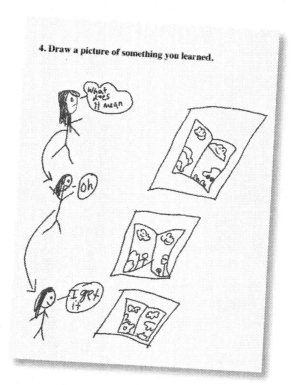

Academic Vocabulary Development

Academic word knowledge is essential for successfully navigating the increasing amounts of complex and informational texts that now play an essential role in literacy instruction. When students create images, "rare words or technical terms receive semantic support" (Heath and Wolf 2005, 38). Visual-based strategies benefit vocabulary development and effective correction of student misconceptions (Paquette, Fello, and Jalongo 2007).

Visual texts may also provide a scaffold for understanding complex terms. For example, textbook publishers often include maps, graphs, and photographs to complement and expand the written definitions of key words and concepts. Cappello and Lafferty (2015) saw an increased use of Tier 2 and Tier 3 words (Beck, McKeown, and Kucan 2002) when using a visual-based curriculum for fourth-grade science instruction. As a result, students used academic vocabulary, such as *luster* and *cleavage*, when writing in their geology curriculum. Students are able to use critical vocabulary in oral and written language outside of reading and describing visual texts. Cappello and Lafferty noticed that "students used the academic vocabulary necessary to communicate their new science thinking around geology" (2015, 291) during other points in the curriculum, even when asked to use more traditional methods for classroom communication. This transfer is important for all students, but the benefits are critical for the English learners in our classrooms.

Certainly, nonlinguistic representations have a positive effect on academic vocabulary learning for our English learners. It is especially important to include illustrations, charts, photographs, maps, and realia to illustrate new ideas and concepts for these students (Marzano, Pickering, and Pollock 2001).

Accountable Talk

Visual texts generate classroom accountable talk, demanding classroom discussions that require students to build on one another's comments with accurate and applicable contributions (Zygouris-Coe 2015). Students learn to make explicit connections to the images and to one another as they expand and deepen understanding. Teachers comment about seeing students respectfully "contradict each other" (Roper, classroom teacher) and learn to build on one another's comments, even when they do not typically contribute to classroom conversations.

There is evidence that accountable talk transfers to student writing (Cappello and Walker 2016). Students build claims based on what they have learned from each other. Figure 1.3 represents a sixth-grade student's analysis of a visual text. The same student's reflection after working with peers is shown in Figure 1.4. Notice the difference in details, as well as the acknowledgment of other students' contributions to his understanding.

TERMS TO KNOW

classroom accountable talk

conversations where students add relevant ideas that enhance overall understanding

MY NOTES:
I think the picture has two imprints of one a foot
print and a car tire print.

The picture shows on the very bottom of the page
a scale to show what the snow depth is.

Figure 1.3 before discussion

GROUP NOTES:
From what I heard from the other students it
appears that a persons foot walk across the snow
and later a car or truck's wheel must have run
over the foot imprint. The bottom of the page
that says snow depth I heard some students say it
might be because they want us to find the depth
of both the imprints. Along with that I spotted a
purple background with snowflakes on the back of
the picture.

Figure 1.4 after discussion

Student Engagement

Teachers want students to be engaged participants in the classroom, encouraging them to question, make connections, and build on ideas. Students must be actively involved in order to benefit from instruction. This is important for all learners but has special implications for students new to English or struggling with literacy. Offering students "multiple ways in which to express and demonstrate meaning" (Albers 2006, 75) is one way to help students focus and is, therefore, a pathway for student success. In addition, "the seemingly contradictory aspects of novelty (new for school) and familiarity (used outside of school) create a setting to support engagement" (Cappello and Lafferty 2015, 292).

Visual- and multimodal-based activities expand students' literacy toolkits, providing choices that enable them to more fully participate in the classroom culture. This has both academic and social outcomes. Students still learning to read and write may excel at viewing and illustrating ideas and concepts, thus enhancing their status within the class. This, in return, motivates further engagement. Visual-based norms in schools are not as clearly articulated as written and oral language communication modes. Therefore, students may focus on the assignment without the weight of standardized performance expectations. Most students were eager to work with visual texts across the curriculum.

"Normally he sat silently in class but the...lesson inspired new classroom behaviors. He went nuts with it. He saw things that I would need a magnifying glass to see. He was participating."
—Roper, classroom teacher describing the change in a student's participation during visual-based lessons

Risk Taking

For some students, active engagement is not sufficient. Students must feel a "welcomeness to engage" (Wood and Harris 2016, 33) in an affirming classroom climate that creates opportunities for academic and social risk taking. Goodwin et al. view risk taking "as an orientation to try or explore something new even though a positive outcome is not guaranteed" (2015, 135). Therefore, risk taking is defined as "students' willingness to engage with a novel instructional tool or take chances when not entirely certain they have correct answers" (Cappello and Lafferty 2015, 292). With fewer school-like expectations and standards established, the use of visual texts may encourage students to take risks with their learning.

Furthermore, lowering the affective filter (Krashen 2008) eliminates factors that may interfere with creating comprehensible input for our English learners and

Reducing Anxiety in a Visual Environment

Discover and observe ⟶ Engage ⟶ Take future risks

risk taking

a student's willingness to engage in learning even when he or she is unsure of the correct response

others with diverse language needs. The affective filter is a psychological barrier to learning created by anxiety or lack of self-confidence. Creating a safe environment for learning and welcoming students to take risks are two of the essential advantages visual texts have for supporting English learners in our classrooms (Cappello and Lafferty 2015; Cappello and Walker 2016; Britsch 2010; Cummins and Quiroa 2012; Wilhelm 1997).

> The visual-based strategies were "big with English learners. I saw a lot of my RSP [Resource Specialist Program] kids too. They were so confident when they were sharing out."—**Kat, classroom teacher**

Anxiety also decreases with visual-based instruction. Why is this important? Low anxiety increases the possibility for learning. For example, using visuals in science classrooms provided a low-anxiety atmosphere to enhance learning. "Students' observations of rich details of photographs help them to share their thoughts with peers, ease their anxiety of learning a new concept, and make them feel comfortable to participate in discussions. During discussions, the students actively sought information from the photographs and used the data to ask and answer questions" (Lee and Feldman 2015, 507). "Photography may also provide less proficient language users a way to safely express their ideas without the fear of failing or measuring up to their peers" (Cappello and Lafferty 2015, 293).

Teachers also comment on the decrease of student anxiety when visuals take the spotlight in the classroom. With less anxiety and more risk taking, teaching with visual texts creates safe spaces for students to take risks within the lesson (Cappello and Walker 2016). Students who rarely contributed in the classroom participated in conversations that focused on visuals. Teachers attributed this to the nature of visual-based instructional settings.

Working with visual texts "made a safe space for the kids who don't normally share because there is no judgment and I never say 'great.' I never use terminology which makes one kid's input better than the other."—Janet, classroom teacher

Ethical Responsibility

With all these articulated benefits to using visual-based literacy strategies, including essential advantages for our English learners, there is an ethical responsibility to teach students to critically view and illustrate ideas through visual texts. One of the most important elements of instruction is providing access to the curriculum. This is an effective approach for teachers looking for equitable ways to meet the literacy needs of all the students in the classroom.

What does this mean? Instruction that is primarily focused on the print word will not meet the needs of all students. A multimodal, visual-based curriculum provides alternative, and perhaps more accommodating and flexible, pathways to access and express curricular understandings (Ranker 2014). Teachers must expand the range of communication tools so students can fully participate in classroom culture and all students, including our language learners, can "fully represent their meanings" (Britsch 2009, 718). Visual-based experiences have the potential to create educational opportunities where "our language abilities do not define the limits of cognition (Eisner 2002, 12). Further, teachers who work with students with special language needs "know that visual tools offer an entryway for all learners into organized mental and language processing. These visuals teach and anchor sequential logic, and mastery of these logical skills leads to the grasping of bigger ideas" (Essley 2010, 45). This has both academic and social outcomes, a truly equitable classroom practice.

Therefore, we encourage teachers and students to utilize all the language arts in classrooms: reading, writing, listening, speaking, viewing (reading images), and visually representing or illustrating (depicting ideas).

example of providing access to resources

Instructional Uses

Like reading, writing, listening and speaking, visual texts have both receptive and productive purposes. When we view images, reading them for understanding, visual texts are used in a receptive mode. Visual texts work as a productive mode when we use them to visually represent, illustrate, and express knowledge. To be clear, in some cases, visual texts are the best communication tool to capture certain kinds of information, and in these cases, they are their own valued literacy.

Recognizing the role of visuals does not diminish the significance of the traditional language arts in education. Images can also be used as scaffolds to support reading and writing. "English language arts learning activities are seldom wholly discrete—just reading, just writing, or just viewing, for example. Each medium relates directly or indirectly to every other" (IRA and NCTE 1996, 5).

Strategies for Viewing

Like reading and listening, viewing visual texts is a receptive mode. Reading visual texts for understanding is now a necessary literacy skill, vital for success in our everyday lives. Outside of school, the world is ubiquitously visual; images are everywhere! Visual texts help us locate directions using a map, make choices based on advertisements, and simplify and summarize critical information in graphs and charts. In school, increased amounts of informational texts across the curriculum also make this call for visual literacy important. Informational texts are loaded with visual elements used to elaborate and complement written text, but are sometimes on their own, critical for understanding. In addition, helping students analytically read and understand visuals is important when considering the amount of digital text they face daily. Electronic text is almost always multimodal, and visual communication is essential in this form of communication. These strategies are effective tools that teach students how to read and understand visual texts:

- Visual Thinking Strategy
- Who Is It?
- Character Clusters
- Prove It!

- Exclusion Brainstorming
- Geometric Reading
- Stepping-Stones
- Common Clues

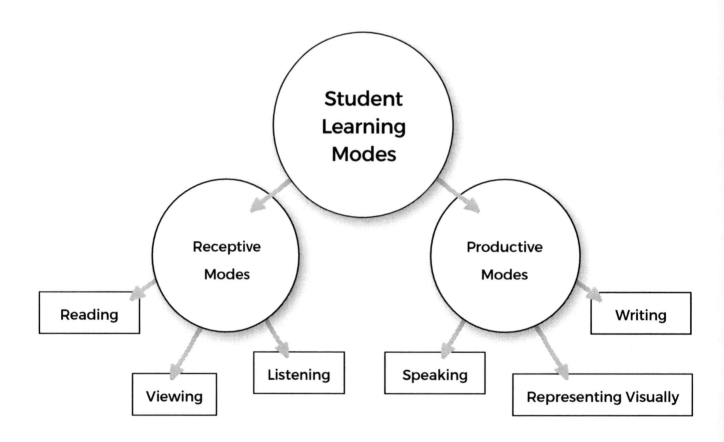

Strategies for Creating

Like writing and speaking, visually representing is a productive mode. Also like writing and speaking, the goal of visual representations is communication.

Students' illustrations should be seen as another language for expressing ideas: one that has fewer school norms and expectations and may be an alternative for students new to school or English. Indeed, visual representations have the potential to create educational opportunities where "our language abilities do not define the limits of cognition" (Eisner 2002, 12).

"Allowing students new or alternative ways to communicate understandings improves learning outcomes by creating varied opportunities for assessment" (Cappello and Lafferty 2015, 288). Student products, such as drawings, graphs, or multimodal texts, demonstrate learning and can help teachers determine whether students have met the lesson objectives. Students will be able to visually illustrate their learning using any of these strategies:

- Talking Drawings
- Collaborative Text Information Maps
- Storyboard
- Excitement Graph
- Listen to Me
- Visual Measurement
- Properties and Categories of Matter
- Classify This!

Using Visuals to Scaffold Traditional Literacies

Sometimes, visual texts and visual strategies scaffold (bridge) traditional literacy skills. Scaffolds are temporary supports created to provide students opportunities to learn difficult concepts (Vygotsky 1978). While the scaffolds are in place, students practice and build confidence. However, these supports are temporary. The goal of these strategies is transfer to traditional literacies. For example, picture books have long been used to teach story grammar, such as character and setting. Students are expected to demonstrate their understanding of story grammar as they read written text and write their own stories.

Planting an apple tree

Step 1   Step 2   Step 3   Step 4   Step

Apple

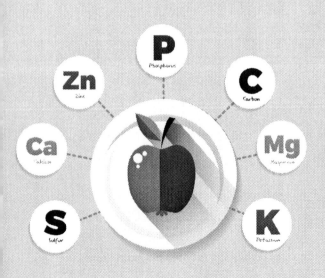

Zn
Zinc

P
Phosphorus

C
Carbon

Ca
Calcium

Mg
Magnesium

S
Sulfur

K
Potassium

Choosing Visual Texts

"I chose images that make [the social studies lesson] more realistic... so they can visualize what actually happened rather than just reading words. The image really broadens their understanding of the topic."

—Jessica, classroom teacher

Just as teachers need to choose appropriate written texts to meet instructional goals, they must also carefully choose visual texts for their lessons. Choosing visual texts is not as simple as it may seem. Deciding which images to include in the curriculum is a complex process—one that is essential for successfully using the strategies that follow. Indeed, not every visual text suits every instructional objective, much in the same way not every written text will meet students' needs. Further, "simply adding images may not be enough to yield the many potential benefits that result from embedding visual texts within the curriculum; images must be carefully selected to serve instructional purposes" (Cappello 2017, 733).

This process may be new for teachers who have grown accustomed to using visual texts as supplemental rather than essential teaching tools. However, as teachers "become more aware of the increasing role of visual communication in learning materials of varying kinds, they are asking themselves what kind of maps, charts, diagrams, pictures and forms of layout will be most effective for learning" (Kress and van Leeuwen 2006, 14).

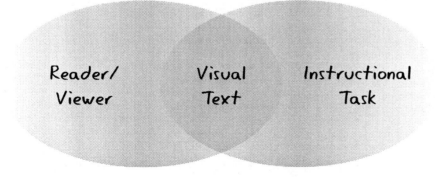

Locating Visual Texts

Since there is need for a range of visual texts to meet a variety of instructional purposes, it is important to have many resources for accessing images for classroom use. Sanctioned classroom textbooks do provide a starting point; however, these commercially available publishers' materials tend to use images that are supplemental to written texts and may not stand strongly on their own. There are also many advantages to using teacher- and student-created images for teaching and learning. Teachers can photograph intriguing items or use graphic organizers to arrange related details in a visual way. However, the wide range of topics that must be covered may make this impractical and limiting. There are many online visual resources that can be leveraged for classroom instruction. Creative Commons is an accessible site for sharing and remixing images that are free from copyright restrictions. In addition, museums often offer free access to their collections for educators.

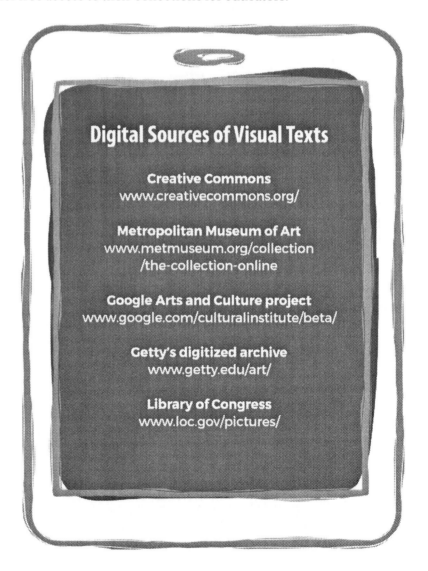

Digital Sources of Visual Texts

Creative Commons
www.creativecommons.org/

Metropolitan Museum of Art
www.metmuseum.org/collection
/the-collection-online

Google Arts and Culture project
www.google.com/culturalinstitute/beta/

Getty's digitized archive
www.getty.edu/art/

Library of Congress
www.loc.gov/pictures/

Factors to Consider

There are many elements to consider when choosing visual texts to include in your curriculum. This process of planning for visual-based strategies is similar to other classroom instruction in which you must consider the standard and/or objective, the task or instructional activity designed to meet the lesson's goal, the student's skill level and literacy characteristics, and the visual text itself with a specific focus on its complexity.

Consider the Objective

The first consideration for teachers is the goal of instruction. What is the purpose of the lesson? What should students take away from this interaction? Lesson objectives should be built from student need. They are also constructed through a close examination of the grade-level literacy standards and expectations. For many of the strategies, additional disciplinary standards were combined to create objectives with measurable and observable student outcomes that provide a way to monitor and assess student learning. Thus, images chosen must align with the lesson or unit objectives. Draw students' attention to specific elements, such as challenging academic concepts or vocabulary.

The instructional objective grounds other considerations: reader/viewer (the student), instructional task (the strategy or activity at the heart of the lesson), and visual text (with particular attention to complexity).

Consider the Instructional Task

The instructional task refers to the lesson activity or strategy in which students will participate. Of course, different tasks require different tools. This is no different from choosing easier written texts for independent reading and more complex texts for guided reading. Similarly, some visual-based strategies require visual texts that are easily read/viewed (such as Listen to Me on page 139) and others require the complexity of multiple layers of interpretation (such as the Visual Thinking Strategy on page 39). When thinking about the task, it is important to consider levels of student engagement.

Consider the Reader/Viewer

No lesson should be planned without the student as the central focus of instruction. The purpose of instruction is to help students stretch to meet academic goals. Lessons must be built with this idea in mind, specifically about the kinds of support that might be offered to help students grow and learn. Therefore, "there is no greater consideration when choosing visual texts for instruction than the student" (Cappello 2017, 736).

Teachers should consider the overall characteristics that influence their visual text choices for their class, such as students' background knowledge and prior experiences, including exposure to visual texts in instructional settings. It is important for classrooms to have a feeling that creates a "welcomeness to engage" (Wood and Harris 2016). An affirming classroom climate creates opportunities for academic and social risk taking. However, teachers must also reflect on students' needs and consider particular literacy characteristics, language development level (including emergent bilingualism), and the specific ways students may benefit from transacting with nonlinguistic representations.

Consider the Knowledge Demands

Teachers must consider and build upon students' academic and personal life experiences when assessing for visual text complexity. What are the students' experiences that they can bring to the viewing of the text? What knowledge of other texts (written or visual) can students bring to understanding this image? Does viewing and understanding the image presume prior specialized or technical knowledge? Is the academic content aligned with what has been previously taught?

Visual-Text Complexity

One way to address the idea of visual-text complexity is to apply the qualitative features of complex written text described (NGACBP and CCSSO 2010) and elaborated on by others (Fisher and Frey 2014; Fisher, Frey, and Lapp 2016; Sierschynski, Louie, and Pughe 2014). This should be done with caution. First, it is important to note that applying these criteria does not imply a call for leveling of visual texts in any way. It would not be authentic or helpful to teachers to have images deemed appropriate for a specific grade or viewing level. As previously discussed, so much more must go into choosing visual texts, including the viewer's needs, lesson objectives, and instructional activities. Second, complexity is not simply a linear idea; it is indeed complex and there are many overlapping characteristics to consider.

In order to combat an implied hierarchy of images, teachers can use the Qualitative Scale of Visual-Text Complexity in Figure 2.1, which is a visual representation of the process of considering visual-text complexity. The elements gather around three big categories (adapted from the four highlighted for considering written text as outlined in the CCSS):

* those elements contributed by author/image-maker
* those found within the visual text
* those brought to the experience by the viewer/reader

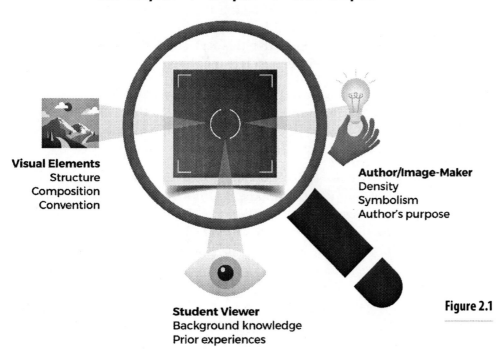

Qualitative Scale of Visual-Text Complexity

Less Complex ➡ Complex ➡ More Complex

Visual Elements
Structure
Composition
Convention

Author/Image-Maker
Density
Symbolism
Author's purpose

Student Viewer
Background knowledge
Prior experiences

Figure 2.1

Author/Image-Maker Considerations

The image-maker cannot be separated from the visual text. We recognize the image-maker in the decisions about structure and conventionality of the visual text, but the role of the creator begins with why the image was created. What is the purpose or intention of the visual text? When considering levels of purpose and determining a visual text's complexity, the three essential elements to explore are density, symbolism, and author's purpose.

Density refers to whether there is a single or literally explicit meaning or if there are ambiguous components that require critique. The density of the visual text affects how it is viewed and the level of support needed.

Symbolism considers the implicit or constructed meanings of the representations in the text. Explore the range of symbols in the image. Does the image-maker use literal depictions, common symbolic representations (a flag for "patriotism" or green for "pastoral"), or nonrepresentational figures that require viewers to draw conclusions about the visual text?

Author's purpose reflects the image-maker's intentions in creating the visual text. Does the image illustrate a concept or supplement written text, or was it created to communicate an aesthetic or intellectual understanding?

Visual Elements Considerations

While exploring the complexity of visual-text structure and conventions cannot be separated from the image-maker, these areas are complex in and of themselves. The elements of the visual text can be explored as compositional features. Although structure and language conventions are sometimes considered separately in other literacy discussions, they are combined in this section because they are best studied as contributions from within the visual text itself.

Structure refers to the image's overall organization and appearance, including medium, composition, and use of supplemental information. Considering complexity through structure includes reflecting on the *visual medium*, including expected or expanded use of materials and techniques of the form.

Compositional features are also paramount to the complexity of an image. Image-makers use a range of approaches from the traditional (e.g., foreground/background) to those that depict subjects in multifaceted or ambiguous perspectives that evoke meaning or emotion. In addition, *supplemental information* is an indicator of visual-text complexity. More complex images are difficult (or impossible) to understand on their own.

Convention is used here to refer to register, the formal or informal variations of visual texts. Within schools, there will still be a range of registers, from scholarly (e.g., transatlantic trade maps) to informal (e.g., student drawings). In exploring complexity of conventions, we determine whether the image communicates with technical/archaic or casual and familiar visual elements.

Student Viewer Considerations

Student viewers must always remain at the core of planning instruction and thus any exploration of visual-text complexity. It is important to remember that conceptions of complexity shift depending on who is examining the visual texts.

Background knowledge can aid with interpretation of visuals. A student who is familiar with the subject of the visual text may be able to more meaningfully make connections to the visuals and make inferences about what the image-maker is communicating.

Prior experiences with similar visual texts can prime students to recognize common symbols or compositional features. A child who has explored many patriotic images of the United States will have a contextualized understanding of the eagle image on the back of a quarter coin.

Example: Choosing a Visual Text

The following section provides a transparent view of the thinking behind making one of these critical choices to best meet the needs of a specific group of second-grade students.

The Lesson: Schools Then and Now

This process of choosing a visual text is for a lesson that is part of a larger unit that emerged from an examination of the social studies and literacy standards at the second-grade level. The overarching standard from history and social studies is "Students differentiate between things that happened long ago and things that happened yesterday" (CSBE 2000, standard 2.1). In addition, English Language Arts standards (for both reading literacy and information text) require that second-grade students "read closely to determine what the text says explicitly and to make logical inferences from it; cite specific textual evidence when writing or speaking to support conclusions drawn from the text" (NGACBP and CCSSO 2010, CCRA.R.1). Specifically, this lesson focuses on the standard "Ask and answer such questions as *who*, *what*, *where*, *when*, *why*, and *how* to demonstrate understanding of key details in a text."

Objective

The lesson's purpose emerged from these guiding standards as well as an evaluation of student needs. Therefore, the specific lesson objective (with measurable and observable outcomes indicated) is as follows:

Students will be able to read the text to make logical inferences from it and cite specific textual evidence to support claims about when the action in the image occurred (yesterday or long ago).

Instructional Task

Since the second graders need support making logical inferences and are learning to cite specific evidence to support claims, the Visual Thinking Strategy (see page 39) is an effective strategy to meet the instructional objective. The nature of the strategy, including the questioning protocol, provides structured opportunities for students to identify evidence to support inferences made based on visual information. These are visual text–dependent questions and align with the standard's requirements. Philip Yenawine, one of the co-creators of the Visual Thinking Strategy (VTS), recommends that teachers choose images for the strategy that are fairly complex, with familiar subjects "so that students have much to recognize, but they also contain elements of mystery so students have observations, ideas, and emotions to puzzle over" (2003, 24). There is a three-question protocol to follow using this strategy:

Visual Thinking Strategy (VTS) Protocol (Yenawine 2013)

- What is going on in the picture?
- What do you see that makes you say that?
- What more is there to find?

Students will identify and differentiate between things that happened long ago and things that happen now, citing evidence from the visual texts.

Readers/Viewers

The first-semester second-grade students in this urban classroom include 40 percent emergent bilingual students who are learning English from home languages, including Spanish and Tagalog. The school neighborhood includes many multifamily homes where three generations typically reside together. The students are very good at identifying literal information in text but are still learning to make logical inferences.

Multiple languages are spoken by students in this classroom, which makes literal knowledge easy to access, but students still need support making inferences.

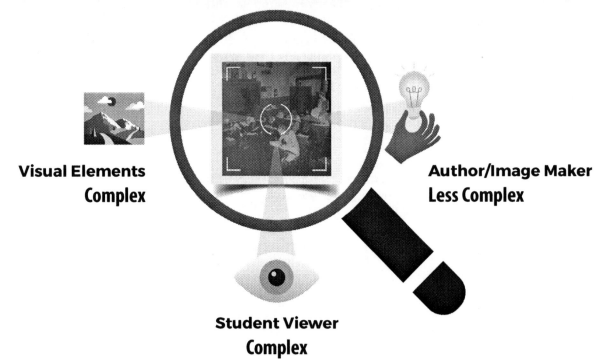

Visual Elements
Complex

Author/Image Maker
Less Complex

Student Viewer
Complex

Knowledge Demands

To accurately identify the information about schools from long ago, students will need to recognize classroom elements that may look different than they do today. They will need to understand that the things they do every day in school can be done in different ways. They must make inferences about tools that do not look familiar. They may wrestle with big ideas about how things change over time. This specific group of students may be well-prepared to talk about *long ago* because of the presence of multiple generations in many local homes. Conversations with grandparents and familiarity with family changes across generations will add to student success.

Students will need a recognition of different ways of doing familiar things, an understanding of change over time, and experience with multi-generational conversations.

Visual Text Complexity

Two potential images were located to support the second graders in this classroom as they worked toward the lesson objective. The Qualitative Scale of Visual-Text Complexity (QSVTC) was a useful tool for assessing the appropriateness of these images for instructional goals. Suggested visual texts for this lesson and their corresponding scales are shared below.

Image One: Photograph of an American schoolhouse

The first image (page 32) was located on Getty Images. This image, taken around 1943, met the general criteria for Visual Thinking Strategy images suggested by Yenawine (2003). Students may recognize the setting as a classroom based on the books and desks. However, there are several elements that require further thinking.

The QSVTC illuminates the levels of complexity. The scale provides a detailed exploration of this visual text's complexity and, therefore, its usefulness for the second-grade context and lesson objective. Overall, this image was found to be moderately complex. This photograph functions to illustrate a school of the past, and the traditional symbols included (books, chalkboard) are reinforcements. Conventional compositional devices, such as the straight-on perspective and use of black-and-white photography, also make this image more accessible. However, this image does not align with modern student life experiences. Because this visual text is only moderately

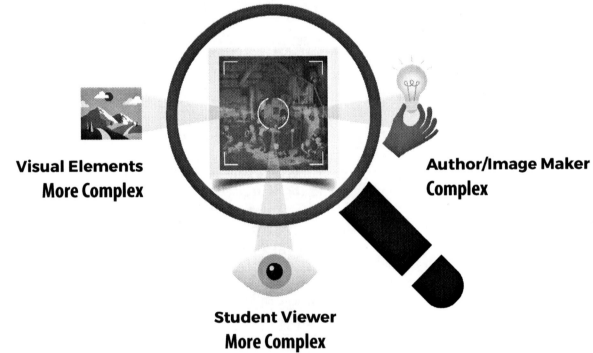

Visual Elements
More Complex

Author/Image Maker
Complex

Student Viewer
More Complex

complex, it might be best used to introduce and practice the Visual Thinking Strategy, an engagement that typically requires higher levels of complexity. This image may also be useful for lesson differentiation and taught to a small group of students in advance of the whole-group activity suggested using the second image.

Image Two: "The Schoolmaster," Adriaen van Ostade (1662)

The second image (page 34) chosen, *The Schoolmaster* (1662) by Adriaen van Ostade, was identified using the Creative Commons website and found at Wikimedia Commons. Although this painting is owned and exhibited at the Louvre Museum, it has entered into the public domain. This image of a school in the past is much more complex and might better serve to expand and elaborate the second graders' understanding.

Once again, the QSVTC was used to detail visual-text complexity. Students might be less familiar with the medium of painting (as compared to photography) and the artistic techniques, such as chiaroscuro (the contrast of light and shade), used to communicate meaning and evoke emotion in this visual text. Since this is a fine art painting, it requires specialized scholarly knowledge and, therefore, is quite complex in register. In addition, the multiple layers of information make this visual text dense. However, the supplemental information (the title) provides support for understanding.

Because this image is significantly complex, it might be more appropriate for a Visual Thinking Strategy lesson for those second-grade students who are learning to cite evidence to support their claims that this image captures action from long ago.

Reflective Questions

1. Why is it important that reading visual texts is explicitly taught in all content areas?

2. How do images increase a student's understanding of material?

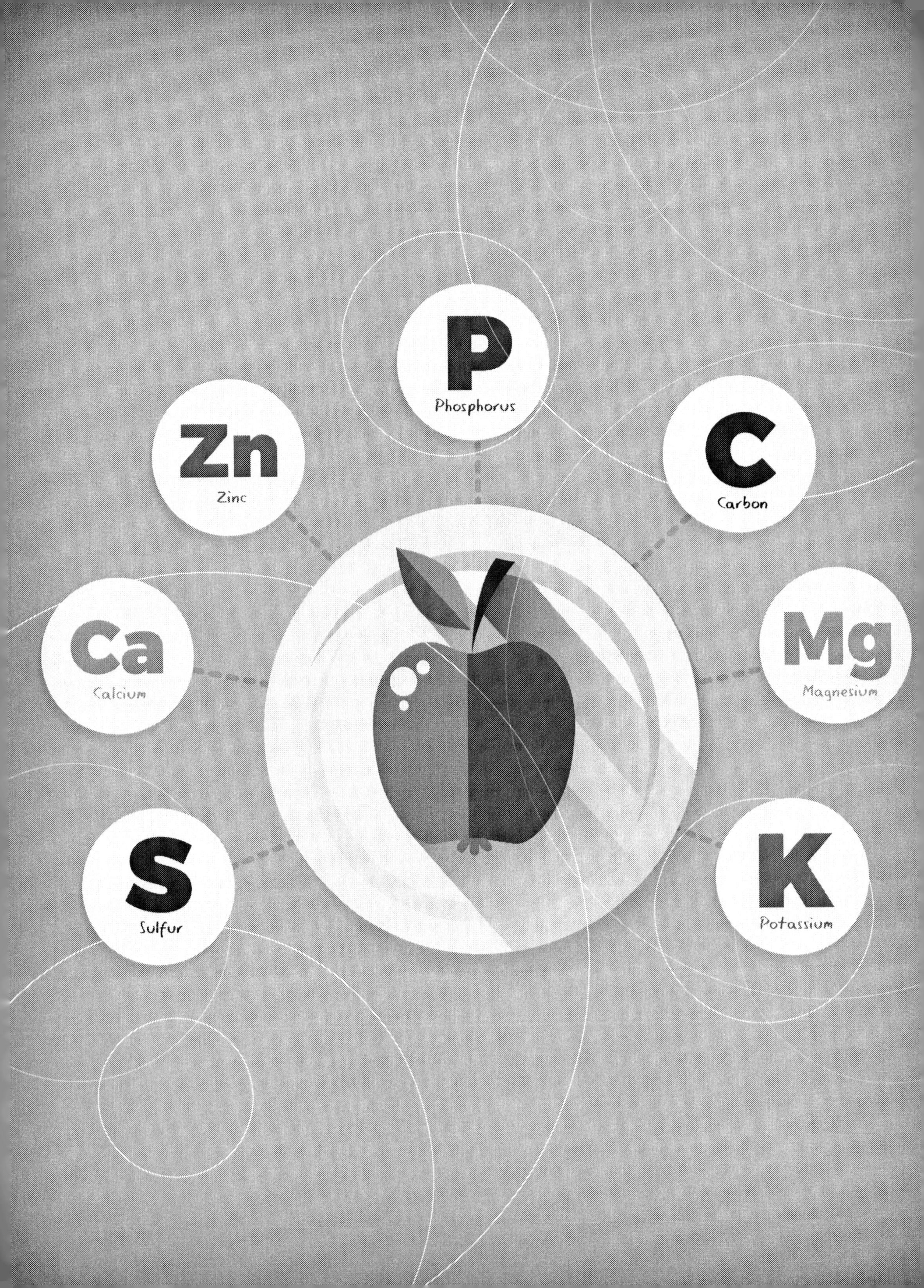
P
Phosphorus
Zn
Zinc
C
Carbon
Ca
Calcium
Mg
Magnesium
S
Sulfur
K
Potassium

Strategies for Viewing

"Not only did they have the support of the picture, but they had the support of one another by hearing what other students saw using that language."

—Jessica, classroom teacher

This section includes instructional strategies and sample lessons for teaching students to read visual texts for understanding. Like reading or listening, viewing is a receptive mode. Also like reading and listening, the goal of viewing images is comprehension.

Note: All objectives are written from the student's perspective using "I Can" statements that help make lesson goals student centered. The statements clearly communicate what students will be able to do after completing the lesson successfully.

Strategies for Viewing

Overview:

The Visual Thinking Strategy (VTS) is a foundational strategy that helps students and teachers learn to examine and analyze a range of visual texts to get to the deeper meaning (Cappello and Walker 2016; Housen 2007; Yenawine 2013). At the core of the strategy is a discussion protocol that capitalizes on the wealth of information found in visual texts for literacy learning across the curriculum. Borrowed from museum education, this strategy can be applied to fine art, photographs, illustrations, maps, and other graphics. The Visual Thinking Strategy can also be used to discuss three-dimensional objects.

Purpose:

The whole- or small-group discussions that emerge during VTS lessons leverage all students' contributions and build upon personal and social knowledge relevant to the image under review. Students learn to lead VTS lessons, using the questioning protocol and highlighting information in the image.

It is one of the most flexible strategies shared in this text and is useful to help meet literacy learning objects in any academic discipline because "VTS does not teach what to think, but rather supports the discoveries students make when they are given opportunities to think in various ways (Yenawine and Miller 2014, 3).

Essential Questions:

The carefully sequenced VTS protocol includes three questions:
1) What is going on in this picture?
2) What do you see that makes you say that?
3) What more can you find?

Quick Ideas by Grade Level:

Grades K–1: VTS can be used to learn academic language around relative locations, including *near/far*, and *bottom/top*, as well as compositional terms, including *foreground* and *background*. VTS can be used to explore different occupations as part of a unit on community.

Grades 2–3: VTS is a great way to start any social studies unit. Use a complex image from the textbook, and guide the discussion to determine what students already know and what needs more robust teaching.

Learning about Learning Long Ago

Objective

I can read the picture and give proof about learning long ago.

Materials

Display a VTS anchor chart of the three-question protocol. Provide images for VTS that are complex in nature with multiple levels of meaning and room for interpretation. Gather them from picture books, novels, and electronic sources, such as the Google Arts and Culture site at **artsandculture.google .com**. The visual for this lesson example is an image of a school from long ago. The image and Visual Thinking Strategy Activity Sheets are located on pages 172–173 in Appendix A and in the Digital Resources.

Time

approximately 20–30 minutes

I DO

In contrast to many of the other strategies in this text, there is no modeling. VTS begins with an invitation to engage students in thinking about the image.

WE DO

1. Provide students about one minute to silently skim the visual text in the same way they would skim written text, moving quickly and lightly. Start at the top left corner. Move top to bottom and left to right.

2. Ask, "What's going on in this picture?" Student answers may include "I think they are students at school" and "I think this photograph is from a long time ago."

3. Ask, "What do you see that makes you say that?" Student evidence may include "I think it is a classroom because there are students at desks, and there is a chalkboard." Point to the place in the image that highlights evidence.

VTS Three-Question Protocol

In this strategy, it is imperative to ask the three questions in this order:

1. What's going on in this picture?

2. What do you see that makes you say that?

   This question requires students to identify the specific content that helped them interpret and decide what is going on in the picture.

3. What more can we find?

   Yenawine (2013) recommends teachers only ask, "What is going on in this picture?" one time at the beginning of the lesson. The question "What more can we find?" helps students build on what has already been discussed as well as dig deeper for more information and analysis.

4. Paraphrase students' ideas for validation. Paraphrasing also offers students another way to express an idea; it may also serve to clarify.

5. Ask, "What more can we find?" Continue to ask this question until students have sufficiently mined the image for details to support their claims.

YOU DO TOGETHER

1. Even as young as kindergarten, students can lead VTS discussions on more familiar topics. For example, once the teacher models leading a discussion using the image on page 172, students work in small groups using additional images related to "Learning about Learning Long Ago."

2. Students use the anchor chart as needed to adhere to the questioning protocol.

3. Have students take turns leading five-minute VTS discussions. When participating in multiple VTS experiences around the same topic (such as Learning about Learning Long Ago), it is important to note similarities and differences among the images.

YOU DO ALONE

1. Have individual students synthesize the information learned about learning long ago. This section explicitly supports the writing standard that students learn to write from sources.

2. Have students use two copies of the VTS Activity Sheet to record their learning from two visual sources.

3. On the back of a VTS Activity Sheet, have students draw or write the similarities and differences between the pictures. This part of the lesson can also be done with the teacher.

4. Independent work may serve as an assessment to monitor student progress toward the objective.

Differentiation for English Learners

- Foster discussion around evidence by providing language frames to hang or post in the classroom.

- When working with emerging English learners, start by listing what you see in the image as a way to build vocabulary. Label items when skimming the text to reinforce word knowledge.

- Label nouns in one color and adjectives (or other parts of speech) in another color.

Writing for Transfer

Students write in graphic organizers to identify their main ideas and supporting details taken from the Visual Thinking Strategy lessons.

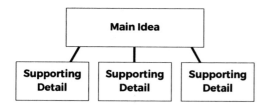

Students write about the drawings they created in the You Do Alone component of the lesson that synthesize information from multiple visual resources. "What was learning like long ago?"

Marva's Classroom Moment

One first-grade classroom compared their classroom to the one in the image. They completed a Venn diagram comparing and contrasting schools then and now, leading to additional written response and teaching about the compare-and-contrast text type.

People Who Make a Difference

Objective

I can identify people from the past who have made a difference in others' lives.

Materials

Provide images for the Visual Thinking Strategy that are complex in nature with multiple levels of meaning and room for interpretation. Gather them from picture books, novels, and electronic sources, such as the Library of Congress or museum collections. The image used at the center of this lesson is *Washington Crossing the Delaware* by Emanuel Leutze in 1851. The image and Visual Thinking Strategy Activity Sheets are located on pages 174–175 in Appendix A and in the Digital Resources.

Time

approximately 30 minutes

I DO

1. In contrast to many of the other strategies in this text, there is no modeling. VTS begins with an invitation to engage students in thinking about the image.

    - **Note:** Starting in second grade, teachers may add quick-writes to a VTS lesson for additional transfer of understanding.

2. Before the discussion protocol, have students quick-write about what they believe is going on in *Washington Crossing the Delaware* by Emanuel Leutze. The three-question protocol posed to the group follows.

WE DO

1. Provide students about one minute to silently skim the visual text in the same way they would skim written text, moving quickly and lightly. Start at the top left corner. Move top to bottom and left to right.

2. Ask, "What's going on in this picture?" Student answers may include "They are in a boat trying to go somewhere, but they are stuck" or "They are in danger in the boat."

3. Ask, "What do you see that makes you say that?" Student evidence may include "I think they are stuck because it is winter and there is ice in the water" and "They are in danger because there are too many people in the boat."

4. Paraphrase students' ideas for validation. Paraphrasing also offers students another way to express an idea; it may also serve to clarify. "You think the people in the boat are in danger because there are too many of them in the boat. Do you think they could also be in danger because of the ice?"

5. Ask, "What more can we find?" Continue asking this question until students have sufficiently mined the image for details to support their claims. Student answers may include "I think they are moving somewhere or getting away from somewhere because they have horses in one of the boats!"

YOU DO ALONE

1. Have individual students synthesize the information from the discussion, and give them another opportunity to quick-write about the image. Encourage students to include the specific ideas learned from the VTS lesson and the resulting discussion in their second writing. "Were your ideas confirmed? Have your ideas changed? Do you have new understanding?"

2. Independent work may serve as an assessment to monitor student progress toward the objective.

Differentiation for English Learners

• Encourage students to take risks and lead VTS discussions. Often English learners have developed strong visual literacies skills as a way to compensate for their struggles with academic language.

• Pull a small group to pre-teach any historical people, events, or vocabulary they may not know.

Writing for Transfer

Students use the quick-write they created after the VTS discussion to initiate a research report or biographical text on important historical figures whose achievements have touched others. The elaborated text should draw upon the information and evidence highlighted in their quick-write. This can be accomplished with annotation—students underline the main idea and put questions marks beside the topics needing additional information.

Integrating Technology

There are several advantages to projecting the image digitally during a Visual Thinking Strategy lesson, including the ability to zoom into specific areas of the visual text when needing to address details. In addition, colors may be important for understanding and are better reproduced digitally than in hard copy. Finally, it is cost-effective to project the image rather than make individual student copies.

- When projecting images, students may request to come up to the screen to point out evidence or clarify ideas. Proximity seems to play an important role in understanding, especially for English learners.

- VTS can also be effective when using smartboard technologies.

- Tablets are especially helpful when students are leading small-group VTS lessons.

Reflective Questions

1. How does a close reading of a visual text encourage finding evidence to support claims made about what is going on in the image?

2. What role do size, color, and compositional placement have in helping understand what the artist is communicating?

SECTION
03

Overview:

Who Is It? is an adaptation of the classic game Guess Who?, created by Ora and Theo Coster. The game was first produced by Milton Bradley and is now owned by Hasbro. The purpose of this game and the strategy adaptation is to be the first player (student) to deduce the mystery character. Students ask yes/no questions to eliminate characters and narrow the pool of possibilities until the mystery character is identified.

Purpose:

Who Is It? teaches students how to effectively use the process of elimination. Logical reasoning is developed as students ask well-crafted questions that focus on descriptive details.

Essential Question:

How can logical reasoning and the process of elimination be used to determine the mystery character?

Quick Ideas by Grade Level:

Kindergarten: Guess My Holiday: Use images that represent holidays, such as Independence Day, Washington's Birthday, Labor Day, and Veterans Day.

Grade 1: Guess My Symbol: Create a game that reviews American symbols and landmarks, such as the flag, a bald eagle, and the Statue of Liberty.

Grades 2–3: Guess My Hero from Long Ago: As part of the biography unit, students design game pieces for their heroes, including Abraham Lincoln, Louis Pasteur, Sitting Bull, Albert Einstein, Golda Meir, etc.

All grades: Students of all grades can become acquainted with the rules by playing the classic Guess Who? game as a means of introduction. There are many seasonal adaptations available online to easily create game pieces related to the social studies standards.

Who Is My Classmate?

Objectives

I can use yes/no questions. I can figure out the mystery classmate.

Materials

To play Who Is It?, use the game Guess Who? to model the strategy. Create a second deck of character cards with content-specific images that are clear and explicit, with multiple and varying descriptive characteristics. The more similarities found in the images, the more challenging the strategy will be. This lesson focuses on Who Is It? using children's photos. The images and Who Is It? Activity Sheet are located on page 176 in Appendix A and in the Digital Resources. There is also a blank Who Is It? for teachers to use with their students' photographs in the Digital Resources.

Time

approximately 20 minutes

I DO

1. Students will have varying experiences with this classic game, so be sure to take the time to model using the traditional game pieces. Use only one game board, and begin with all the game pieces raised up and in view.

2. Say, "I have chosen a mystery character from this deck of 24 faces. It's your job to ask me yes/no questions to figure out my chosen character. For example, I may ask, 'Does your character have brown hair?' If the mystery character has brown hair, then I turn down all the pieces who do not have brown hair. If the mystery character does not have brown hair, then I turn down all the characters who do have brown hair."

3. Demonstrate by turning down all the appropriate game pieces. Repeat with additional yes/no questions.

WE DO

1. Have students practice asking yes/no questions. "What other yes/no questions can we ask about hair?"

2. Provide nonexamples. Say, "'What color is your character's hair?' is not a yes/no question. Remember, I can only answer *yes* or *no*."

3. Give students the opportunity to revise their questions to fit the yes/no format.

For example, if a student asks, "What color is your character's shirt?" they can revise it and ask, "Is your character wearing a blue shirt?"

4. Have students take turns coming up to the game board to turn down the appropriate characters.

5. Use the process of elimination until the mystery character is solved.

YOU DO TOGETHER

1. Say, "Now, we are going to play a special version of the game. This time, you will ask yes/no questions to determine our mystery classmate." Lead the game again, this time using the custom deck of character cards. Begin with all the game pieces in view.

2. Play the game in the same manner. Students ask yes/no questions, emphasizing logical reasoning. Ask, "What questions will eliminate the most classmates?"

3. Guide students to ask questions that move beyond physical representations in the image to include behavioral aspects. Ask, "Does this person play jump rope at recess?"

4. Have students collaborate to determine which game pieces to turn down or leave standing.

5. Have students take turns coming up to the game board to turn down the appropriate classmates that do not have the guessed feature.

6. Continue until the mystery classmate is solved.

If students find it challenging to create yes/no questions or revise their open-ended questions, they can ask friends to help them.

YOU DO ALONE

1. Place students in pairs to play the game using the two-player rules from Guess Who? Students try to solve the mystery classmate before their partners do. To play in pairs, each student will have their own game board with identical character cards arranged in different order.

2. Have them take turns asking yes/no questions and use the process of elimination until the mystery character is solved.

3. Allow students to play multiple times, picking a new character for each round.

Differentiation for English Learners

• Ask students to focus on using descriptive and detailed language.

• Group cards with many overlapping characteristics together to make the mystery simpler to solve.

• Use a smaller deck of 12 to 18 cards rather than the full deck of 24.

Writing for Transfer

Young students write lists of their most effective yes/no questions to guide participation in future games. Sentence frames available for reference on an anchor chart provide additional support if needed.

"What _____ is your character's _____ ?"

"Does your character _____ ?"

Who Is at Work in Our Community?

Objectives

I can match physical traits and jobs to people in our community. I can figure out who the mystery worker is.

Materials

To play Who Is It?, use the game Guess Who? to model the strategy. Create a second deck of character cards with content-specific images that are clear and explicit, with multiple and varying descriptive characteristics. This lesson focuses on government occupations in the community. The deck of 24 character cards includes firefighters, postal carriers, police officers, judges, and members of the military. Be careful to include images that represent gender and ethnic diversity. The images and Who Is It? Activity Sheet are located on page 177 in Appendix A and in the Digital Resources. There is also a blank Who Is It? for teachers to use with their students' photographs in the Digital Resources.

Time

approximately 30–40 minutes

I DO

1. Students will have varying experiences with this classic game, so be sure to take the time to model using the traditional game pieces. Use only one game board, and begin with all the game pieces raised up and in view.

2. Say, "I have chosen a mystery character from this deck of 24 faces. It's your job to ask me yes/no questions to figure out my chosen character. For example, I may ask, 'Does your character have brown hair?' If the mystery character has brown hair, then I turn down all the pieces who do not have brown hair. If the mystery character does not have brown hair, then I turn down all the characters who do have brown hair."

3. Demonstrate by turning down all the appropriate game pieces. Repeat with additional yes/no questions.

WE DO

1. Have students practice asking yes/no questions. Ask, "What other yes/no questions can we ask about hair?"

2. Provide nonexamples. Say, "'What color is your character's hair?' is not a yes/no question. Remember, I can only answer *yes* or *no*."

3. Give students the opportunity to revise their questions to fit the yes/no format.

For example, if a student asks, "What color is your character's shirt?" they can revise it and ask, "Is your character wearing a blue shirt?"

4. Have students collaborate to determine which game pieces to turn down or leave standing.

5. Continue using the process of elimination until the mystery character is solved.

YOU DO TOGETHER

1. Say, "Now, we are going to play a special version called 'Who Is at Work in Our Community?' This time, you will ask yes/no questions to determine our mystery local government worker." (Be sure the game pieces are randomly placed and not clustered by occupation, gender, or ethnicity.)

2. Lead the game using the custom character cards. Remind students of play rules and procedure. You may model one more question if necessary. Ask, "Does your worker wear a uniform?" Students ask yes/no questions, emphasizing logical reasoning.

3. Guide students to ask questions that move beyond physical representations in the image to include aspects of their jobs. Examples may include, "Does your worker spend most of their time indoors?" Students collaborate to determine which game pieces to turn down or leave standing.

4. Have students take turns coming up to the game board to turn down the appropriate occupations that do not have the guessed feature. Continue until the mystery local government worker is solved.

How to Be a Good Guesser

Elicit responses from students to create an anchor chart about how to make a good guess.

- Think about what makes the characters similar or different.

- Start with general questions and move to specific.

- Pay attention to details so you turn down the right pieces.

- Remember to only ask yes/no questions.

YOU DO ALONE

1. Place students in pairs to play the game using the two-player rules from Guess Who? Students try to solve the mystery occupation before their partner. To play in pairs, each student will have their own game board with identical character cards arranged in a different order.

2. Have them take turns asking yes/no questions and use the process of elimination until the mystery worker is solved.

3. Allow students to play multiple times, picking a new worker for each round.

Differentiation for English Learners

- Provide lists of characteristics to help form yes/no questions, including hair color, hair length, gender, glasses, clothes/uniform color, tools, etc.

- Group cards with many overlapping characteristics together to make the mystery simpler to solve.

- Use a smaller deck of 12 to 18 cards rather than the full deck of 24.

- Consider pairing students with different strengths when working together.

Writing for Transfer

Students choose one of the occupations depicted to write about (firefighter, postal carrier, military member, police officer, or judge). Their paragraphs must include the details highlighted in the yes/no questions asked during the Who Is It? Strategy. Students may also be asked to find additional information about their chosen government occupation using the images in the game to guide them.

Who Is It?
Wrap Up

Integrating Technology

There are several free online versions of the Guess Who? game that can be played on tablets or projected into the classroom. Hasbro also offers several free character sheets, including Kooky Creatures, Dinosaurs, and Sports versions. Others have created custom sets of character cards with various themes and varying levels of complexity.

Reflective Questions

1. What does looking at an image of a person or character reveal about their occupation?

2. How does a reader's visual knowledge help form yes/no questions?

Overview:

Character Clusters are built upon the long-used approaches of semantic webs and concept maps, which visually represent relationships and connections as knowledge is collectively constructed. Students use expressive vocabulary to list qualities and attributes of the character found only in the visual text. The strategy requires students to identify the specific pictorial elements that justify their claims about the character. Either teachers or students may transcribe students' ideas.

Purpose:

Specifically, this strategy provides a way for students to organize character traits and other relevant information drawn from a close reading of a visual text. Students identify and use descriptive vocabulary as they analyze key characters in fiction or nonfiction texts. A Character Cluster is an efficient prereading strategy for introducing a specific picture book, read-aloud novel, or character study. A complex image of the character is centered on a blank page.

Essential Question:

What evidence can you find in the visual text that will help you describe and understand this character?

Quick Ideas by Grade Level:

Kindergarten: Students replicate facial expressions or gestures of the character depicted in the cluster. They then use oral language sentence frames, such as the following:

"Look at me! I am _____ ."

"You can tell I am _____ because _____ ."

Grade 1: After viewing additional images (and reading or listening to text pages), students return to the Character Cluster to check accuracy of the traits listed.

Grade 2: Students create three categories on the Character Cluster: what the character says, what the character does, and what the character thinks.

Grade 3: Multiple images of the same character from different parts of the written text can be used to track character changes over time.

All grades: Students create Character Clusters of themselves (see image). This is great as a prewrite or for back-to-school night where parents have to guess which set identifies their child.

My Character Traits
helpful funny independent smart
responsible stubborn
CARING sneaky happy

Learning About Fictional Characters

Objectives

I can read to figure out what the visual text says about a character. I can give proof to support my claims about the character.

Materials

Gather images from picture books, novels, electronic sources, or other related and complex images. Characters depicted in settings add an additional layer of information. Student drawings may also be used for visual analysis. This lesson example explores an image of Cinderella. The image and Character Clusters Activity Sheets are located on pages 178–179 in Appendix A and in the Digital Resources.

Time

approximately 20–30 minutes

I DO

1. Display the complex Cinderella image so that all students can see it clearly. Use an "I stance" (page 57) when modeling. Students do not yet know the character is Cinderella.

2. Say, "From looking at this image, I think the character is worried." Write *worried* on the poster outside the image boundary. It is important for students to see the image as well as the words transcribed by the teacher.

3. Provide evidence to support this claim. Point to the character's face. "I think she is worried because of the expression on her face.

This is what I look like when I am worried. Does it look like the character's face?" List two to three more key traits obtained from the visual text around the image using descriptive language in callouts.

4. Use the background or setting of the image to provide additional clues toward understanding the character. "I see she is on stairs. The way she is going down the stairs looks like she is in a hurry." Make sure to point out the visual evidence to support each claim.

WE DO

1. After several character traits are modeled, have students follow the model and contribute to the discussion. Be sure to elicit appropriate descriptive vocabulary.

2. "I think she is a princess because she is wearing a crown or a tiara." Elicit additional evidence to support claims when available. "Is there anything else that makes you think she is a princess?"

3. Be sure students are using descriptive vocabulary to identify traits. If needed, ask for paraphrases or synonyms. "Is there another way we can say that?"

4. Direct students to write key words to remember their descriptions. For example, "Write *hurrying* here on the bottom near her feet."

5. Students may record their ideas on their own Character Cluster Activity Sheet.

YOU DO TOGETHER

1. Place students in pairs, rereading the visual text to provide additional evidence to support a claim. "Read this picture again, and look closely for any details that may help us understand why she is rushing or in a hurry."

2. Guide students to have discussions using oral-language prompts. Language frames may be used, provided as a handout or hung in the classroom.

   - When one student suggests an attribute ("I think she is happy."), the partner responds with "How do you know?" ("I know because she is smiling.")

   - Have students work together to expand ideas for the same character under development or with another character from the same text. In the example provided, this may be completed with a Cinderella character from another culture.

I Stance

Teachers use the "I stance" when modeling to demonstrate relevant literacy moves they use in their own practice (e.g., "I always start reading images in the top left corner, the same way I do with written text"). This is different from describing the practice, which is most commonly found in classroom instruction (e.g., "You start reading images in the top left corner.").

YOU DO ALONE

1. Independent practice includes time for students to expand their list of character traits.

2. Have students develop word scales or word strings to increase understanding. For example, if the class notes that Cinderella is hurrying, students may add synonyms, such as *rushing* and *running*.

3. Have students draw upon the information in the Character Cluster to write a caption, sentence, or paragraph describing the character based on the visual information.

4. Independent work may serve as an assessment to monitor student progress toward the objective.

Differentiation for English Learners

- Have students circle or highlight the relevant details in the image. Provide the word that names the detail.

- Provide a word bank or use classroom word scales for additional support.

- Foster discussion by providing language frames to hang or post in the classroom. Examples may include:

    "I know she is _____ because _____ ."

    "For example, the artist showed _____ ."

Writing for Transfer

Students use the Character Cluster as a prewrite to create a Missing Person Poster.

1. What attributes listed would help us find the missing character?

2. How might we design the poster using words and images to best get people's attention?

Marva's Classroom Moment

Sometimes, prior visual knowledge and experience may work against comprehension. Be sure to clarify misconceptions.

Student 1: Look, she fell out of her shoe when she was running!

Teacher: That's an important detail. Do you know any characters who lost a shoe?

Students: Cinderella!

Student 2: That can't be Cinderella because her dress isn't blue.

Teacher: How do you know she wears a blue dress?

Student 2: That's what she wears in the movie.

Learning About Historical Figures

Objective

I can read closely to figure out what a visual text says directly about a historical person. I can give proof from the visual text to support my thinking. I can infer what the text says about the same person indirectly.

Materials

Provide images from picture books, novels, electronic sources, or other related and complex images. Characters depicted in settings add an additional layer of information. Student drawings may also be used for visual analysis. This lesson example explores the historical figure George Washington Carver. The image and Character Clusters Activity Sheets are located on pages 180–181 in Appendix A and in the Digital Resources.

Time

approximately 30–40 minutes

I DO

1. Identify the historical figure, and find a complex visual text worthy of close reading. Social studies standards may provide some guidelines.

2. Display or project the image of George Washington Carver so that all students can see it clearly. Remember to use "I stance" (page 57) when modeling. Students do not yet know the historical figure.

3. Say, "From looking at this image, I think this person is some kind of scientist." Write *scientist* outside the image boundary. It is important for students to see the image as well as the words transcribed by the teacher.

4. Provide evidence to support this claim by saying, "I think he is a scientist because the photograph shows that he is using a microscope, and I know scientists use microscopes."

5. Model and list two to three more key traits obtained from the visual text around the image using descriptive language in callouts. Use details from the setting to provide additional clues toward understanding the character. Make sure to point out the visual evidence to support each claim.

WE DO

1. After a few character traits are modeled, engage students in the discussion. Be sure to elicit appropriate descriptive vocabulary.

2. Possible student responses may include "I think this is a person from long ago because it is a black-and-white photo." Be sure students are using descriptive vocabulary to identify traits. If needed, ask for paraphrases or synonyms. "Is there another way we can say that?" "This is a historical photograph." Write *historical* on the border.

3. Elicit additional evidence to support claims when available. Ask, "Is there anything else that makes you think this is a historical photograph?" One possible answer is "I think he is from long ago because I don't see any computers."

4. Have students record their ideas on their own Character Clusters.

YOU DO TOGETHER

1. Place students in pairs to read the picture again and look closely for any details that may help them learn more about the person in the photograph. Language frames may be used, provided as a handout or hung in the classroom.

   - When one student suggests an attribute ("I think he is experimenting."), the partner responds with "How do you know?" ("He is trying different things. It looks like he is trying to get it to work.")

   - Have student pairs organize the callouts into two categories: Physical Characteristics (what the character looks like) and Behavioral Characteristics (what the character does). Everything listed in the Behavioral category must begin with a verb.

2. Have students work together to expand ideas from the same image or with a different picture of George Washington Carver.

Often when students work in small groups, it is a good idea to give them different color markers to highlight individual contributions. Students take pride in their offerings, and it provides the teacher with a way to hold each person accountable and monitor student progress toward the lesson objective.

YOU DO ALONE

1. Independent practice includes time for students to expand their list of character traits.

2. Have students apply their learning to a new person and independently complete Character Clusters.

3. Instruct students to draw upon the information in the Character Cluster to write a caption, sentence, or paragraph describing the person based on the visual information.

4. Independent work may serve as an assessment to monitor student progress toward the objective.

Differentiation for English Learners

• Create additional Character Clusters to develop deeper understandings of the historical figure. For this example lesson on George Washington Carver, resources are listed in Appendix C.

• Provide a word bank or use classroom word scales for additional support. All these resources can include visuals and written texts.

• Foster discussion around evidence by providing language frames to hang or post in the classroom. Examples may include:

"For example, the artist showed _____ ."

"I know she is _____ because _____ ."

"I think this character is _____ ."

"According to the picture _____ ."

Writing for Transfer

Character clusters can be used as a prewriting activity to organize essential character traits before writing about fictional characters or biographical figures.

Integrating Technology

Grades K–1

- Students and teachers can create basic Character Clusters using PowerPoint and Keynote, which both have built-in callout features.

- Students may use apps such as Inspiration, which was created to organize information and create beautiful visual digital Character Clusters.

Grades 2–3

Students can import the character or historical figure into a graphic novel or comic strip that illustrates what the character might say. Comic Life and Strip Generator are two programs that are easy to use with young children.

Reflective Questions

1. How does looking at an image of a historical figure or fictional character reveal what that character feels and thinks?

2. What are the visual elements in the image that help a reader analyze character or behavioral traits?

Overview:

The Prove It! Strategy helps students find and name very specific evidence to justify their conclusions or inferences about a visual text. Complex images often contain information not clearly or explicitly depicted. Therefore, visual texts can be great tools to teach students how to draw conclusions based on what is implied or hinted at through composition, organization, and content. This strategy follows a close reading of the image or the Visual Thinking Strategy (see page 39). It is a companion strategy to Character Clusters (see page 55) and is often used to focus deeply on character analysis.

Purpose:

Prove It! can be used for every story element, so students become fluent in providing evidence to answer any question. Prove It! is a great approach to practice drawing conclusions in both fiction and nonfiction visual texts when details are not explicitly stated—a skill that may be later applied to more traditional classroom texts, such as picture books, textbooks, or novels.

Essential Questions:

What conclusions and inferences can be made about this photograph? What evidence is there to support any conclusions and inferences?

Quick Ideas by Grade Level:

Kindergarten: When focusing Prove It! on setting, teachers may use images of their school site or community.

Grades 1–3: Once students become proficient at finding evidence to support claims in images, they can Prove It! from written texts. Instead of listing the specific pictorial elements that justify conclusions, students list page numbers, paragraphs, or direct quotes from text.

All grades: Create an anchor chart of language used to Prove It! by eliciting ideas from students and finding examples in classroom written texts. The anchor chart can continue to grow throughout the year. Whenever students hear or see ways authors, artists, and peers use evidence to Prove It!, language can be added to the chart displayed. Consider completing the anchor chart using interactive writing.

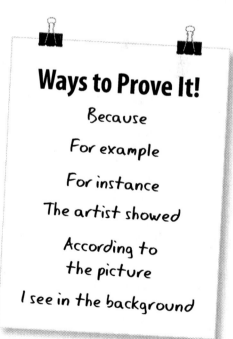

Ways to Prove It!

Because

For example

For instance

The artist showed

According to the picture

I see in the background

Prove It!
Language Arts **K–1**

Setting

Objectives

I can give proof using this visual text to support my thinking about setting.

Materials

Prove It! is best completed when connected to a larger text or unit of study. This example lesson uses an image of a Mexican farm and a U.S. city and was created to support comprehension of the book *Dear Primo: A Letter to My Cousin* by Duncan Tonatiuh. The book focuses on two cousins, one on a farm in rural Mexico and the other in an urban U.S. city. The images and Prove It! Activity Sheets are located on pages 182–183 in Appendix A and in the Digital Resources.

Time

approximately 20–30 minutes

Think-Aloud Strategy

The Think-Aloud Strategy was designed to support second-language learners as they become metacognitive and monitor their own comprehension while reading text (McKeown and Gentilucci 2007). Although not explicitly created for reading images, the Think-Aloud Strategy can be applied to model how readers self-regulate their understanding. This "nondirective approach" requires readers to pause and explore the text, making their thinking—in this case the process of drawing conclusions—explicit.

I DO

1. Introduce the lesson by saying, "This picture represents one of the places our story takes place." Do not explicitly name the setting, rural Mexico. First, examine the picture closely to find clues. Using a pointer or finger, read the image top to bottom.

2. Talk through reading using the Think-Aloud Strategy. Remember to use "I stance" (page 57) when modeling. Be explicit about the literal depictions in the image. "I think this takes place in a hot location. This photograph shows people wearing hats. Also, the land looks very dry because it is crumbly and nothing is growing there."

3. Pause at any confusing places in the image. Say, "I notice in the background the ground looks different. There is a lot of green and things are growing."

4. Make a concluding statement that reveals important information about the setting. List at least one conclusion in the "Best Guess" column on the Prove It! graphic organizer, and provide corresponding evidence.

WE DO

1. Direct students to search for additional evidence to support the teacher's conclusion on setting. "Can you find anything else in the picture that lets us know it is hot?"

2. Students may challenge the conclusion as long as there is evidence to support their claim.

3. Have students draw additional conclusions about the setting. "I think the donkeys are helping them get ready to plant." "I think it is a farm, and they are planting crops."

4. Guide the class to draw a conclusion about the setting using all the evidence and best guesses listed on the Prove It! chart.

5. Encourage the use of accountable talk to build upon one another's contributions.

Accountable Talk

"I want to build upon what Marisol said..."

"I respectfully disagree with Kate..."

"I agree with Damon when he inferred..."

"I have a different inference."

"The evidence tells me something different from what you see, Dr. Marva."

YOU DO TOGETHER

1. Have students practice Prove It! using another image. In this first-grade lesson example, students also read an image of a large urban U.S. city because it is the second main setting in *Dear Primo: A Letter to My Cousin.*

2. Address any nonexamples, and redirect from nonrelevant information to specifically highlight evidence that will help us draw

conclusions about the setting. Ask, "What does that tell us about where and when this image took place?"

3. Have students make and record conclusions about the second setting and provide evidence to support their claims on their Activity Sheets.

YOU DO ALONE:

1. Have individual students find one more additional piece of evidence that helps understand setting.

2. Have students review all the "Best Guesses" and draw conclusions about the setting of the second image.

3. Independent work may serve as an assessment to monitor student progress toward the objective.

Differentiation for English Learners

- Use Prove It! as a companion to the Character Cluster to extend and record specific evidence found in the visual text.

- Have students highlight or circle the location of evidence in the image. This can easily be done by projecting onto a whiteboard, under a document camera, or on individual visual texts provided to students.

- Read *Dear Primo: A Letter to My Cousin* by Duncan Tonatiuh aloud at any point in this lesson to provide additional support.

Writing for Transfer

Use Prove It! to launch a unit about writing conclusions. The language frames below provide additional support as well as the Ways to Prove It anchor chart on page 63.

"I think the setting is _____ because _____ ."

"I conclude the setting is _____ . According to the picture _____ ."

Finding Evidence in Visual Texts

Objectives

I can infer *who*, *what*, *where*, *when*, and *why* by using evidence in the photograph.

Materials

Provide complex visual texts from picture books, novels, textbooks, or electronic sources. This example lesson uses an image from the Getty Collection, *Self-Portrait with Newsboy* by Lewis Hine (1908). The image and Prove It! Activity Sheets are located on pages 184–185 in Appendix A and in the Digital Resources.

Time

approximately 30 minutes

Discussion Prompts

"I wonder"

"I'm confused by"

"The picture shows me"

"How might I figure out"

I DO

1. Model reading the photograph using the Think-Aloud Strategy. Remember to use "I stance" (page 57) when modeling. Be explicit about the literal depictions in the image. Say, "I see this young boy in the middle of the image, but I'm not sure what he is doing."

2. Use prompts to unveil the strategy and deepen student engagement and thinking.

   - "I wonder who the boy is."
   - "How can I figure out where he is? I think that might be a clue to understanding what's going on."
   - "I'm confused by what he is holding."

WE DO

1. Invite students to help solve the problems posed by making inferences based on support in the image. Ask questions such as, "Who can help me figure out what he is holding?" and "Where do you think the photograph was taken?" These questions are always followed with "How do you know?"

2. Work together to find additional elements in the photograph that support inferences. Remind students that the more proof they can find, the more likely their inference will be correct.

3. Complete the Prove It! inferences column under a document camera or on chart paper, so students can see the words and still refer to the large projected image.

 Marva's Classroom Moment

Student 1: I infer that this picture is from a long time ago.
Teacher: How do you know?
Student 1: Because it is in black and white.
Teacher: You're right. There was a time when the only photos we had were black and white, but sometimes we make black and white photographs today. So let's look for more evidence to be sure. Is there anything else that supports our inference that this photograph was taken a long time ago?
Student 2: I see an old-fashioned camera.

YOU DO TOGETHER

1. Place students in small groups to find evidence for inferences suggested by a classmate. "I infer the boy is a mail carrier." "How do you know?" Students study the image for proof that he is a mail carrier and record their ideas on the Prove It! evidence column.

2. Have small groups share their ideas. Record their contributions of new evidence while students make notes on their individual Prove It! charts. Students' lists may include "wearing a uniform" and "standing near a mailbox."

3. Small groups must also work through dissenting ideas. Some differences might be, "I don't think he is a mail carrier. I infer he is a newspaper boy because he is holding a newspaper. Look how big it is!" "I infer he is someone famous. Why would someone be taking a picture of him?"

YOU DO ALONE

1. After several inferences have been made and proof recorded on the Prove It! charts, have students write captions about the photograph. Almost every image (photograph, chart, map, etc.) in textbooks has a caption. Reference textbook pages if needed. Captions are important for photojournalists too.

2. Transcribe students' captions onto sentence strips, hang them around the image, and display this in the classroom.

3. Independent work may serve as an assessment to monitor student progress toward the objective.

Writing Captions

- Captions must be accurate.
- Captions usually tell the main idea about an image.
- Captions may include additional information about something not shown in the image.
- Captions are always written in present tense.
- Do not use terms like "in the foreground" or "the photographer shows."

Differentiation for English Learners

- Pull a small group to pre-teach Lewis Hine's work using the camera for social reform and to change child labor laws in the early 1900s.
- Gather 5 to 10 examples of images with captions. Discuss with students how the captions help explain the pictures.

Writing for Transfer

Students use the evidence collected on the Prove It! graphic organizer to write arguments about their claims about the photograph. Paragraphs should include Prove It! language, such as *because* or *for example*, to make their case to the reader.

Prove It!
Wrap Up

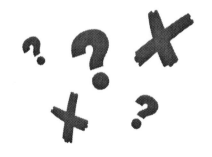

Integrating Technology

The Prove It! Activity Sheet can easily be uploaded to be completed using smartboard or tablet technology in the elementary classroom.

Grades 2–3

Students search the Library of Congress or Getty Archive to find additional Lewis Hine images or other images of children working that help validate their claims made about *Self-Portrait with Newsboy*.

Reflective Questions

1. How does closely reading an image help readers draw conclusions and make inferences about time and place (setting)?

2. What are the pictorial features that may help readers reveal when and where images are created?

Overview:

Exclusion Brainstorming helps students access their background knowledge and make predictions about a topic using fiction or nonfiction texts (Blachowicz and Fisher 2010). Provide a new twist to this strategy by having students discuss what they know about the topic from a close reading of a visual text. Prior to the instruction of a math element, students are presented with a series of complex images for close reading and using vocabulary. They identify the images that relate to the math element and eliminate those that do not belong. Students have the opportunity during the brainstorming process to adjust their hypotheses. Once the lesson is completed, students review the images again to confirm their initial choices and provide justification.

Purpose:

Specifically, this strategy provides a way for students to build background knowledge and mathematical academic vocabulary by brainstorming during the prereading stage of the lesson. This strategy requires students to discuss attributes of the images, activate background knowledge, apply vocabulary, and identify a purpose for reading the image.

Essential Question:

What evidence can be found in these images that will help predict and identify the math objective?

Quick Ideas by Grade Level:

Kindergarten: Students look around the classroom for objects that match the math objective and share with a partner those that can be excluded.

Grades 1–3: After viewing selected shapes, students brainstorm and eliminate those that do not match the chosen shape for study. Students write about their findings and use academic language in their justifications.

Exclusion Brainstorming
Mathematics **K-1**

Learning About Numbers

Objective

I can find evidence in the image that identifies numbers from 0 to 5.

Materials

Gather 15 to 20 images with items that can be counted. Most of the images should have groups of five. Some images and the Exclusion Brainstorming Activity Sheets are located on pages 186–187 in Appendix A and the in Digital Resources.

Time

approximately 20 minutes

I DO

1. Model reading the images using "I stance" (page 57) with a focus on the number 5. Note how much can be learned about the number 5 from closely reading this photograph with several objects in it.

Nancy's Classroom Moment

Encourage students to justify their responses.
Student 1: There are four flowers.
Nancy: That's right. We only see four flowers. Why is this image different?
Student 2: But there are not enough flowers; they need one more flower.
Student 3: We need to add one more flower to make 5.

2. Use the Think-Aloud Strategy to talk about the image. Provide evidence to support the claim. Say, "Looking at this photograph, I count five trees. I also see grass and a blue sky." Remember to use "I stance" when modeling. Write the number 5 on the side of the photograph. Students must see the objects in the photograph as well as the number that they represent.

3. Examine a photograph that does not contain five objects. Say, "I only see four flowers in this photograph. This photograph does not match the other photograph. I will cross out this photograph for elimination." Proceed with the remaining two photographs, making decisions of whether they fit the number 5 or not.

4. Make a conclusion by revisiting the group of photographs, and confirm by checking those that relate to the number 5 and crossing out the photographs that are unrelated.

WE DO

1. Have students closely read the next set of photographs and contribute to the discussion about the number 5.

2. Have the class work together to determine whether the evidence in each photograph supports their claims.

3. Record (based on student discussion) images that support the number 5, and cross out those photographs that need to be excluded.

4. Encourage students to cite evidence in the discussion. Ask, "How do you know the objects in this photograph represent the number 5?" A possible answer may be "I know this because I count five leaves in the photograph."

YOU DO TOGETHER

1. Have student pairs continue to identify photographs supporting the number 5.

2. Encourage students to provide evidence in each photograph that supports the lesson objective.

YOU DO ALONE

1. Have individual students closely read another set of photographs that support the number 5.

2. Have students record by checking photographs that support the topic and crossing out those that do not fit.

3. Have students draw upon the information in the Exclusion Brainstorming to make predictions about the lesson.

4. Independent work may serve as an assessment to monitor student progress toward the objective.

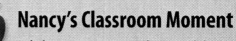 **Nancy's Classroom Moment**

It is important to make careful choices about photographs. Make sure the photograph clearly supports the lesson objective.

Student: Look at the trees. I see five trees, but there is a tree in the front of the photo. And another tree behind the five trees.

Nancy: That's an important detail that you noticed in the photograph.

Differentiation for English Learners

- Have students use a five frame for scaffolding by dropping a token in each box as they count to visualize the concept.

- Foster discussion around evidence by providing language frames to hang or post in the classroom.

  "I know that this is the number _____ because the photograph has _____ trees."

- Encourage oral language development by having students take their Activity Sheets home and explain to their parents or siblings what they saw in the photographs and why certain photographs were crossed out.

Writing for Transfer

Exclusion Brainstorming is the perfect platform for students to write a prediction about the math lesson. Look around the classroom and write a sentence with the number 5. "I see 5 windows." If students are still learning to write, they can draw a picture with five objects. Have students return to the original set of photographs to confirm predictions. Students complete the sentence frame "I crossed out these photographs because they have _____ objects."

Learning About Shapes

Objectives

I can recognize rhombuses, rectangles, and squares as examples of quadrilaterals. I can find evidence of these shapes in a painting.

Materials

Gather 10 images, with half of them depicting quadrilaterals. Student drawings may also be used for visual analysis. Some images and the Exclusion Brainstorming Activity Sheets are located on pages 188–189 in Appendix A and in the Digital Resources.

Time

approximately 20 minutes

I DO

1. Model close reading of a painting that may or may not contain quadrilaterals using "I stance" (page 57). Discuss how much can be learned about the shapes from closely reading the images.

2. Pose prompts that encourage student engagement. Say, "Looking at these paintings, I notice these shapes. Some of these shapes have four sides, and two of the sides are equal."

3. Explain that one painting does not belong in the group. Provide evidence to support why this painting does not belong with the group.

Say, "I think this painting does not belong because the sides are unequal."

4. Check the paintings that relate to the quadrilateral, and cross out the painting that needs to be eliminated.

5. Revisit the list, and confirm by checking the paintings that have quadrilaterals and crossing out the paintings that are unrelated.

WE DO

1. Have students brainstorm the next set of images focusing on the quadrilateral and contribute to the discussion.

2. Find elements in the paintings that support the claims about the images. Ask students to elaborate by using descriptive language. "I see four sides, and some of the sides are equal."

3. Complete an Exclusion Brainstorming by recording (based on student discussion) images to check and cross out.

Nancy's Classroom Moment

Encourage students to closely analyze the paintings that are displayed on the screen. This may involve having them walk up and closely analyze the paintings.
Teacher: Take a closer look at the paintings. Which paintings contain the shape that we have been discussing?
Student: Student walks up to the screen and points to the first painting. "This painting fits because it has a shape with four sides, and two sides are the same size."

YOU DO TOGETHER

1. Place students in pairs to identify paintings, highlighting the quadrilateral shape.

2. Guide student pairs to take on roles by using oral-language prompts. One student asks, "How do you know this is a quadrilateral?" The partner responds with supporting evidence by stating, "I know this is a quadrilateral because _____ ."

3. Allow students to share with the rest of the class.

4. Have students individually write a sentence that states which painting needs to be crossed out and why. Sentences can be shared and confirmed with each other.

YOU DO ALONE

1. Have individual students work on the last set of paintings that support the quadrilateral shape and decide which paintings do not contain the quadrilateral.

2. Encourage the class to draw upon the information in the Exclusion Brainstorming to make predictions about the geometric shape.

3. Independent work may serve as an assessment to monitor student progress toward the objective.

Differentiation for English Learners

- Provide vocabulary words that describe the objects in the painting. English learners can then check the paintings that support the topic.

- Give students pattern blocks to pick out four-sided figures that reinforce the shape and provide justification.

- Have students sort shapes into categories of quadrilaterals, triangles, and squares.

Writing for Transfer

- Exclusion Brainstorming is a great way to encourage predictions about lesson content and using evidence to support a claim.

- Use your classroom as another source for shapes. Provide an opportunity for students to locate quadrilaterals in their classroom or playground environment and write about them in their math journals.

Student Resources: Mathematics Journals

Individual student math journals are a classroom tool designed to support students as they practice and apply mathematics skills. Math journals also provide a way to incorporate writing and metacognitive reflection on the learning process.

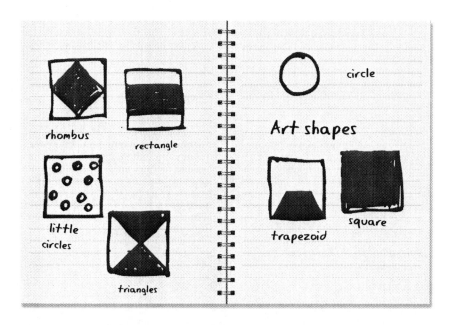

example of a math journal

Exclusion Brainstorming
Wrap Up

Integrating Technology

Grades K–1

- Working individually or with a partner, students can review math sequences by creating counting images using the Starfall app.

- Build the pattern 5 with virtual pattern blocks on interactive whiteboards at **nlvm.usu.edu**.

- Sheppardsoftware.com is a great tool to access primary math games for K–2 (counting 1 to 5 and 1 to 10).

Grades 2–3

- Review and reinforcement of quadrilaterals and other shapes can be found in the "quadrilateral shape shoot" game at **www.sheppardsoftware.com**.

Reflective Questions

1. How does looking at the image allow readers to analyze the attributes of shapes or to understand numbers?

2. How does looking at the image promote discussion of integers, promote discussion of shapes in general, or allow readers to differentiate shapes?

Overview:

Geometric Reading helps students deepen their understanding about a math topic by closely reading a visual text. Visual texts are a great source for making connections with real-world math images. Students are introduced to the math element using a series of complex images for close reading and use vocabulary to identify those images that represent the math element. Geometric Reading provides students with the opportunity to incorporate discussion of math elements in the images, activate background knowledge, apply vocabulary, and identify a purpose for reading the image.

Purpose:

This strategy provides a way for students to activate background knowledge and vocabulary of a math element by observing an image and brainstorming during the prereading stage of the lesson. They have the opportunity to discuss their understanding of the math element and provide evidence to support their claim.

Essential Question:

How do real-world images help students identify, describe, and categorize shapes?

Quick Ideas by Grade Level:

Grades K–1: Use Geometric Reading in a classroom scavenger hunt to allow students in pairs or small groups to look for shapes in the classroom that match the math element.

Grades 1–3: Once students become proficient in Geometric Reading, they can locate shapes in a variety of images and provide evidence to support their claims using oral and written language.

Identifying and Describing Basic Shapes

Objectives

I can point to and describe shapes (squares, triangles, and rectangles) in the image.

Materials

Gather 10 to 15 real-world images that include multiple shapes. Some images and the Geometric Reading Activity Sheets are located on pages 190–191 in Appendix A and in the Digital Resources.

Time

approximately 20 minutes

I DO

1. Display or project a complex photograph containing triangles, rectangles, and squares so that students can see it clearly.

2. Model reading the image top to bottom and left to right. Note how much can be learned about shapes from closely reading the photograph.

3. Use the Think-Aloud Strategy and provide evidence to support your claim. Say, "Looking at this photograph, I can see shapes with three sides and four sides."

4. Provide evidence to support that the photograph contains shapes. Point to the photograph, and begin to identify the evidence using markers. Say, "I see five triangles in the image. I am going to outline

🍎 Nancy's Classroom Moment

Encourage students to search for other shapes in the photograph and justify their responses.

Teacher points to a rectangle.

Teacher: Do you know this shape?

Student 1: It's a rectangle!

Teacher: That's right. Why is this shape different from a square or triangle?

Student 2: The sides are different.

Student 3: They don't match like the square.

them in yellow. I see three rectangles, and I am going to outline them in blue. I see two squares, and I will outline them in red."

5. Use the background or the setting of the image to provide additional clues toward understanding the image.

6. Remember to point to and discuss the evidence that supports the shape of a triangle, rectangle, or square. There must be visual evidence to support the claim.

WE DO

1. Work together to locate shapes and contribute to the discussion. Be sure to elicit appropriate academic vocabulary.

2. Record (based on student discussion) shapes in the images to support triangles, rectangles, and squares.

3. Guide students to cite evidence in the discussion. "How do you know this image has a triangle?" "I know this because the shape has three sides."

YOU DO TOGETHER

1. Have students continue to identify images and walk to the board to outline them in appropriate colors: triangles in yellow, rectangles in blue, and squares in red. Be sure there are enough shapes on the board so that all students have an opportunity to participate.

2. Encourage students to provide evidence from each photograph that supports the topic.

YOU DO ALONE

1. Have students work independently to closely read another photograph that contains triangles, rectangles, and squares.

2. Have students record their evidence by outlining the shape of a triangle, rectangle, or square using the appropriate color.

3. Independent work may serve as an assessment to monitor student progress toward the objective.

Student Resources: Math-Based Literature

Children's literature provides another opportunity for Geometric Reading and can easily be incorporated into a math lesson. For example, *Shapes* by Judith Nouvion and *Cubes, Cones, Cylinders, & Spheres* by Tana Hoban reinforce the attributes of shapes with captivating photography. For young architects and engineers, *The Story of Buildings* by Patrick Dillon provides plenty of opportunities for students to practice Geometric Reading as they learn about the history of famous buildings around the world.

Differentiation for English Learners

- Have students trace shapes and observe colors to provide an opportunity to compare and contrast attributes of the shapes and share their learning.

- Encourage oral language by having students take their Activity Sheets home and explain to their parents or siblings what they saw in their photographs and why certain shapes were colored.

Writing for Transfer

A classroom shape hunt provides students with an opportunity to locate shapes in their learning environment. Have students look around the classroom and write a sentence with the shape. Display language frames with math vocabulary and pictures of the shapes in your pocket chart as scaffolds for the writing experience. In addition to writing, students can draw a picture of the shape in the classroom. Language frames can be compiled into a class book.

I see a _____ (shape) in the window.

I see a _____ on the table because it has _____ sides.

I know the door is a _____ because it has four sides.

Categorizing Shapes

Objectives

I can find evidence in the text to group shapes. I can place them in different categories (rhombuses, rectangles, and others).

Materials

Gather 10 complex, real-world images that contain a variety of shapes, such as triangles, squares, and rhombuses. Some images and the Geometric Reading Activity Sheets are located on pages 192–193 in Appendix A and in the Digital Resources.

Time:

approximately 20 minutes

I DO

1. Model close reading of a photograph using "I stance" (page 57) that contains a variety of shapes.

2. Begin discussion that encourages student engagement. Use the Think-Aloud Strategy and say, "Looking at this photograph, I notice shapes. Some of these images have four sides, and two of the sides are equal."

3. Provide evidence to support that the photograph contains shapes. Point to the photograph. Say, "Here is a triangle. I am going to outline it in yellow. I will check this image for other shapes. I see three rectangles, and I am going to outline them in blue. I see two squares, and I will outline them in red."

4. Remember to point to the evidence that supports the shape of a triangle, rectangle, or square. There must be visual evidence to support each claim.

WE DO

1. Guide students to contribute to the discussion of the photograph and their observation of the shapes.

2. Work together to locate additional shapes and use math vocabulary when describing the images. Ask students to elaborate. "I see four sides, and two of the sides are equal."

3. Complete Geometric Reading by outlining (based on student discussion) the shapes in the photograph.

YOU DO TOGETHER

1. Place students in pairs to work to identify shapes in the photograph.

2. Have student pairs share their evidence with other groups at their table.

3. Encourage students to take roles by using oral-language prompts. One student can ask, "How do you know this is a quadrilateral?" The partner can respond with supporting evidence by stating, "I know this is a quadrilateral because _____ ."

YOU DO ALONE

1. Have individual students work to finish identifying and highlighting shapes in the photograph.

2. Direct students to reflect in their math journals using words and shapes to describe key learnings.

3. Independent work may serve as an assessment to monitor student progress toward the objective.

Differentiation for English Learners

- Have students glue cutouts of shapes to grid paper to create a building and deepen their understanding of how shapes work.

- Have students complete a 4-Corner Vocabulary Chart for vocabulary reinforcement with a partner or in small groups.

Writing for Transfer

Provide an opportunity for students to locate shapes in their classroom or playground environment. Have students design their own building on grid paper using shapes that were discovered in the photograph and write justifications using academic language.

Student Resources: Vocabulary Graphic Organizer

The 4-Corner Vocabulary Chart was designed to build academic language and can be used in math to deepen understanding of concepts (Vogt and Echevarría 2008). English Learners require multiple opportunities to work with academic language in oral language and in writing. This strategy can be used in all grade levels and across content areas and provides a scaffold for writing.

Vocabulary Word	Sentence
Rectangle	My window is a rectangle.
Definition	**Illustration**
A rectangle is a plane with four sides and four right angles.	

Integrating Technology

Grades K–1

- Students can use virtual pattern blocks on their interactive whiteboards to build shapes at **nlvm.usu.edu**.

- Students may use sites such as **www.sheppardsoftware.com** to access the Shapes Shoot game where they can move the target shape into a matching shape.

Grades 2–3

- Splash Math is a set of powerful math apps students can use to review attributes of quadrilaterals with different orientations.

- Students can practice their skills with geometric shapes using virtual elastics on the Geoboards web app.

Reflective Questions

1. How does reading an image provide opportunities for students to categorize shapes?

2. How does reading an image promote the use of academic language in a discussion of shapes and their characteristics?

Overview:

We first heard about the Stepping-Stones Strategy during a presentation by our colleague Dr. Douglas Fisher and later read more about it at Discovery Education. We have effectively used this strategy for vocabulary development as well.

In this next section, the Stepping-Stones Strategy has been extended to support scientific disciplinary literacy in additional ways and more specifically as a way to recall information made from observations in media to construct an account or explanation.

Purpose:

This strategy requires students to organize visual or multimodal information before, during, and/or after viewing a brief clip. This strategy also increases engagement by focusing attention on the video during viewing. The completed Stepping-Stones mat then serves as a scaffold for constructing an oral or written scientific account or explanation, or for addressing a scientific question.

It is important to remember that videos, like written texts, are structured to reflect different text types—*descriptive* and *taxonomic reports*, *procedural* and *procedural recount* text types as well as *sequential explanations*. Stepping-Stones is well designed to provide scaffolding for understanding all these common text types in science videos.

Essential Question:

How can one recall information gathered from observations in media to determine patterns in the natural world or account for natural phenomena?

Quick Ideas by Grade Level:

Grades K–1: Create a Stepping-Stones mat in a pocket chart so that it can be reused with many different video clips.

Grades 2–3: Stepping-Stones can be completed with multiple visual passes. The first pass might be for explicit information and vocabulary building. Additional passes may include inferences. Include nonexample Stepping-Stones with images or written text that are not excerpted from the clip.

All grades: This flexible strategy can be used to launch a unit and frontload key vocabulary. Students listen for the key terms in short clips introducing a science topic. It can also be used to recall information at the end of a unit. Students complete their Stepping-Stones Strategy as an authentic assessment.

How Do Seeds Travel?

Objectives

I can look at video to learn scientific information. I can explain how seeds travel.

Materials

Gather one to two images of stepping-stones to help students visualize what they are when you introduce the strategy. Choose very explicit and well-sequenced video texts that run between one and four minutes in length. For this example lesson, the two short videos shown were about what a plant needs to survive and how seeds travel. In addition to the video, Stepping-Stones requires screenshots or captures, a Stepping-Stone mat large enough for students to see (best if laminated for reuse), and written text (optional). The images for the second video and Stepping-Stones Activity Sheets are located on pages 194–195 in Appendix A and in the Digital Resources.

Time:

approximately 15–20 minutes

I DO

1. Explain and show images of stepping-stones to highlight the process of this strategy. Say, "Stepping-stones are used to help get from one place to another when we have to cross over or through challenges. Today, we are going to use Stepping-Stones to help us get to our goal: recalling information about plants."

2. "We are going to use pictures or screenshots from a video to help us get to our goal. As we watch the video, we will lay the pictures down on the Stepping-Stone mat to help organize and remember the information in the video."

Marva's Classroom Moment

After using this strategy several times in a first-grade class, I intentionally put the pictures in the incorrect order. Students eagerly corrected me, heightening engagement. This also models risk-taking behaviors for students emerging into literacy.

3. Model the strategy with the first one-minute video about what a plant needs. First, lay out the five images, each representing what a plant needs to live (water, space, air, soil, and sun). Use the Think-Aloud Strategy (on page 64) to model thinking about the images.

4. As the video plays, order the images on the Stepping-Stone mat. Students must see both the video and the process of organizing the images. Pause the video after the first image, and make sure students understand the process. "Why did I put this image on the first stepping-stone?"

5. Say, "I think I have these in the right order, but I want to watch again to make sure." Watch the video clip a second time to determine that the pictures are in the right order.

WE DO

1. Say, "Now it's your turn to try." Distribute materials, including the Stepping-Stones mat, pictures, and a set of written sentences in envelopes for each student. This step can be completed individually, but students work more successfully at this stage in pairs or trios.

2. Have students review each image as it is placed on their desks. They make predictions about the topic of the video or the order in which the images will appear.

3. Begin the next video about how seeds travel, and model with the first stepping-stone. Pause the video after the first image, and make sure students understand the process. Say, "Why did I put this image on the first stepping-stone? Do you have the same image on your Stepping-Stones mat?"

YOU DO TOGETHER

1. Have students continue to place images on their Stepping-Stones mats as the video progresses. Pause the video, if needed, to help students confirm their organization.

2. Allow students to talk with each other to check their work at the end of the video. Students can revise the image order on the mats or make any additional changes.

3. Watch the video again to help students validate their organization. Say, "Watch one more time to make sure you have organized all the ways the video shows how seeds travel."

YOU DO ALONE

1. Have students organize their own sets of written text strips to match up with the order of the images on the Stepping-Stones mat.

2. Watch the video a final time to make sure the words match the images. Both the words and images are presented in the video.

3. Independent work may serve as an assessment to monitor student progress toward the objective.

Differentiation for English Learners

- Use the video as a text for science and as a tool for differentiation itself. Strategically pair students to best provide support for English learners.

- Vary the number of images required for students to organize onto their Stepping-Stones mat.

- Pull a small group to frontload the pattern in the video text. "_____ helps seeds travel."

- Prepare students for the video by completing a picture walk and reading *TIME for Kids® Good Work: Plant Life* (available in English and Spanish).

Writing for Transfer

Stepping-Stones can be used as a prewriting strategy. Once students have organized their visual information, they can write in paragraph form or in a graphic organizer to further demonstrate understanding. Have students use the pattern gathered from video observations to explain the natural phenomena of how seeds travel. Sentence and paragraph frames provide support for the pattern "_____ helps seeds travel."

Animal Families

Objectives

I can observe video to learn scientific information. I can compare young animals to human babies.

Materials

Gather one or two images of stepping-stones to help students visualize what they are when you introduce the strategy. Choose very explicit and well-sequenced video texts that run between one and four minutes in length. The video about animal families used in this lesson came from the Everyday Learning Collection of PBS.

In addition to the video, Stepping-Stones requires screenshots or captures, the Stepping-Stones mat large enough for students to see (best if laminated for reuse), and sentence strips. The images for this lesson and Stepping-Stones Activity Sheets are located on pages 196–197 in Appendix A and in the Digital Resources.

Time

approximately 30 minutes

I DO

1. Explain and show images of stepping-stones to highlight the process of this strategy. Say, "Stepping-stones are used to help get from one place to another (your target or goal) when we have to cross over or through challenges. Today, we are going to use Stepping-Stones to help us get to our goal: recalling information about animal babies."

2. "We are going to use pictures or screenshots from a video like stepping-stones to help us get to our goal. As we watch the video, we will lay the pictures down on the Stepping-Stones mat (see page 197) in the order they

   appear. This will help us stay organized and remember the information in the video."

3. Distribute materials, including the Stepping-Stones mat, screenshots, and a set of written texts in envelopes for each student. This step can be done individually or in pairs or trios.

4. Have students review each image as it is placed on their desks. Make predictions about the topic of the video or the order in which they will appear.

5. Start the video, and model the process. Identify the first image, and place it on a large Stepping-Stones mat. Students must see both the video and the process of organizing the images. Pause the video after the first image, and make sure students understand the process. "Why did I put this image on the first stepping-stone?"

WE DO

1. "Now, it's your turn to try." Continue the video. "When you see the next Stepping-Stone, raise your hand."

2. Pause the video after the next Stepping-Stone to monitor student engagement and success. Say, "Does everyone have the same image placed on their Stepping-Stones mats?"

YOU DO TOGETHER

1. Have student pairs continue to place images on their Stepping-Stones mats as the video progresses. Pause the video, if needed, to help students confirm their organization.

2. Have student pairs talk with each other to check their work after the video has ended. Students can revise the order on their mats or make any additional changes.

3. Watch the video again to help students validate their organization. "Watch one more time to make sure you have organized all the baby animals."

4. Have students write the gist of the video after working together.

YOU DO ALONE

1. Have each student write his or her own set of sentence strips to align with the order of the images on the Stepping-Stones mat. Sentences may restate or elaborate on the visual information on the stepping-stone. For example, they may provide information that compares each animal baby to a human baby.

2. Watch the video a final time to make sure the words match the images. Both the words and images are presented in the video.

3. Independent work may serve as an assessment to monitor student progress toward the objective.

Differentiation for English Learners

- Create an anchor chart of signal words that help readers notice the ways things are the same and different (e.g., *alike, same, similar, different, however, but, yet*).

- Provide additional support by using the alternative group of Stepping-Stones that is multimodal located in the Digital Resources.

Writing for Transfer

- Choose one stepping-stone to write about.

- Students conduct research and organize their information using a Venn diagram.

- Students write comparative text structures to compare one baby animal to a human baby.

Stepping-Stones
Wrap Up

Integrating Technology

There are many online options for sources of educational videos for this strategy, including free and paid subscriptions.

- Local PBS stations have many resources for teachers.

- **National Science Teachers Association** ngss.nsta.org/ngss-videos.aspx

- **Discovery Education** www.discoveryeducation.com

- **Generation Genius** www.generationgenius.com

Reflective Questions

1. How do the Stepping-Stones help readers move through challenges to get to the goal (understanding)?

2. What images from the video made the biggest impact?

Overview:

Common Clues is an effective way to introduce a science or social studies unit of study. The benefits of this approach for launching a unit include opportunities to both assess and build student background knowledge on disciplinary themes and topics. This complex task begins in kindergarten. Another benefit the Common Clues Strategy provides is support for literacy learners who are required to gather and integrate information from multiple print and digital sources in order to answer a question.

Purpose:

Using this strategy, students view and discuss a series of increasingly detailed and specific images. They search for, find, and identify the common pictorial elements and content highlighting patterns among the images. These shared features become the clues that help students draw conclusions and make predictions about the new science unit.

Essential Questions:

What similarities and patterns can be identified in multiple visual texts to support conclusions about science themes and topics? How do these patterns help make predictions about a science unit of study?

Quick Ideas by Grade Level:

Grades K–1: Students select an image from an image bank that they believe also has the Common Clues to add to the series.

Grades 2–3: Students search the web and classroom library for additional images that also have the Common Clues.

All grades: Common Clues is an engaging strategy that also may be constructed as a classroom game. Table partners compete to be the first to use the clues and predict the unit of study.

SECTION 03

Common Clues
Science K–1

Offspring Survival

Objectives

I can predict the next science unit using visual texts.

Materials

Provide a series of at least five increasingly detailed and complex visual texts (paintings, drawings, photographs, and other graphics) drawn from picture books, textbooks, and electronic sources. The images must be sequenced from vague to specific in order to help students draw conclusions. The six images in this lesson sequence focus on what parents do to help their offspring survive. The images and Common Clues Activity Sheet are located on pages 198–199 in Appendix A and in the Digital Resources.

Time

approximately 20–30 minutes

I DO

1. Say, "Today, we are going to look at a series of pictures that will help us make predictions about what our next science unit will be." Examine the first image carefully using the Think-Aloud Strategy, and draw attention to specific elements of the visual text. Details are important because the goal is to find what the images have in common.

2. Say, "This is a photograph of some bears. There are three bears in the image, one is much bigger than the others. I notice the sky is blue in the background. I don't know if this is an important detail, but the big one is looking down at the little bears. That could be a clue."

3. Project and explore the second image. Notice the similarities and differences between the two images. Point out the clues the two images have in common.

4. Say, "First of all, they are both photographs, so that is something similar, and it could be a clue. Also, there are three ducks in this picture and three bears in the first one. Plus, ducks are animals too."

WE DO

1. Have students review and restate the similarities between the two images. List clues on a chart or the whiteboard for easy reference as all six images are explored. Look for these clues in the third image.

2. Say, "Let's look at the third image. First of all, this image is a photograph too, so that still could be a clue. But there are no birds in this photo. Who can help me find what this image has in common with the other two?"

3. Return to the first two images for review as needed. Accept all logical responses that can be supported by evidence. Perhaps the zebra is being fed. Perhaps all three images show mothers and children.

YOU DO TOGETHER

1. Project the fourth image. Students turn and talk with their neighbors or table partners about what common clues they can find in all four images. These clues will lead to a conclusion.

2. Say, "Tell your partner all the things these pictures have in common. These are our clues, and they will help us make a prediction about what our next science unit will be about."

3. Say, "Think carefully about what this unit might be about. Who has a prediction?" Elicit responses. Ask for evidence to support any claims about the unit of study.

4. Finally, display the fifth and sixth images of the series. Discuss how the clues in the image may confirm or challenge their ideas about what the unit will be.

5. Ask, "Does this picture match or strengthen your prediction?"

YOU DO ALONE

1. Have students complete the Common Clues Activity Sheet to provide evidence of their conclusions. They will list their conclusions about the theme and provide evidence by drawing or writing in the magnifying glass.

2. Independent work may serve as an assessment to monitor student progress toward the objective.

Differentiation for English Learners

- Practice Common Clues in a small-group setting using a different topic to give students experience in making predictions.

- List the similarities of the images on a chart or the whiteboard during the lesson. Add to the list, and delete clues when they do not appear in subsequent pictures.

Writing for Transfer

Have students create foldable books of all the images used in the Common Clues lesson. Each image must be captioned or elaborated upon with writing. Students continue to build their books as the unit unfolds, adding pages when they learn more ways parents care for their offspring.

Animal Adaptations

Objectives

I can predict the next science unit using visual texts.

Materials

Provide a series of at least five increasingly detailed and complex visual texts (paintings, drawings, photographs, and other graphics) drawn from picture books, textbooks, and electronic sources. The images must be sequenced from vague to specific in order to help students draw conclusions. It is helpful to arrange images in a slideshow for easy projection. The six images in this series focus on animal adaptations. The images and Common Clues Activity Sheet are located on pages 200–201 in Appendix A and in the Digital Resources.

Time

approximately 30 minutes

I DO

1. Say, "Today, we are going to look at a series of pictures that will help us make predictions about what our next science unit will be." Using the Think-Aloud Strategy, draw attention to specific elements of the visual text. As the concepts grow more complex, emphasize the common clues.

2. Say, "This is a photograph of giraffes. They seem to be on the plains somewhere in the wild, and it is very dry. I notice the giraffes are reaching their very long necks up to a tall branch. I know they are herbivores, so they eat leaves and plants. That is why they have long necks, to be able to eat the high leaves."

3. Project and explore the second image. Notice the similarities and differences between the two images. Identify the clues the two images have in common.

4. Say, "First of all, they are both photographs, so that is something similar, and it could be a clue. Also, the first image is of giraffes, and this one is of elephants, and they both look like they are in their natural habitat. I know they are both mammals, so that is something in common. Elephants also eat plants, so they're alike in that way too."

WE DO

1. Have students review and restate the similarities between the two images. Explain that these are the clues for finding similarities in the third image. They may be charted to provide extra support.

2. Say, "Let's look at the third image. This one doesn't have some of the clues in the first two. First, sharks are not mammals. They are fish. Mammals are air breathing, and sharks don't breathe air. Sharks and other fish have *gills* that help them breathe underwater. What does this image have in common with the other two?"

3. Return to the first two images for review as needed. Accept all logical responses that can be supported by evidence. Perhaps the images show natural habitats. Perhaps they show them eating and drinking.

YOU DO TOGETHER

1. Project the fourth image. Say, "Tell your partner all the things these pictures have in common. These are our clues, and they will help us make a prediction about what our next science unit will be about." Students turn and talk with their neighbors or table partners about what common clues they can find in all four images. These clues will lead to a conclusion.

2. Say, "Think carefully about what our unit might be about. Who has a prediction?" Elicit responses. Ask for evidence to support any claims about the unit of study. Often at this point, students believe the unit is about habitats because that is a common clue. Invite other possibilities. Say, "Turn and talk to your partner again to find any other common clues."

3. Finally, display the fifth and sixth images of the series. Discuss how the clues in the image may confirm or challenge their ideas about what the unit will be. This final image of a chameleon helps make clear the theme of animal adaptations.

4. Say, "Does this picture match and strengthen your prediction?"

Signal Words for Writing Comparisons

 same

 alike

 similar

 also

 likewise

 in comparison

YOU DO ALONE

1. Have students complete the Common Clues Activity Sheet to provide evidence of their conclusions. Students will list their conclusions about the theme and provide evidence by drawing or writing in the magnifying glass.

2. Independent work may serve as an assessment to monitor student progress toward the objective.

Differentiation for English Learners

- Practice the strategy in a small-group setting before the whole-group activity. Use a different topic, but provide experience making predictions based on the common clues found in multiple visual texts. This also provides the advantage of proximity, as students can handle and more closely read the images in a small-group setting.

- Provide additional support by listing the similarities on a chart or the whiteboard as you move through all the images. You can add to the list and delete clues when they do not appear in subsequent pictures.

Writing for Transfer

Have students create foldable books of all the images used in the Common Clues lesson. Each image must be captioned or elaborated upon with writing. Students continue to build their books as the unit unfolds, adding pages when they learn more ways that animals can adapt.

Integrating Technology

- It is easy to project and move among the images if they are organized and presented in PowerPoint, Google Slides, or Keynote.

- Students can learn to use reverse image search to find their original source and additional information by dragging the image into the search bar on **www.google.com**.

Reflective Questions

1. What approaches work best when closely reading images to find Common Clues?

2. How does discovering visual-based clues aid in making predictions?

Strategies for Creating

"I took a lot of pictures and wrote a lot. I loved taking pictures...It was sort of hard but still easy. I would want to do this again. I loved to used the camera, and I don't really like writing. But I liked these stories."
—Barbara, elementary school student

This section includes instructional strategies for guiding students to visually illustrate understanding. The focus is on visually representing. This means that the visual-based strategies in this section specifically target support for improving reading and writing.

Note: All objectives are written from the student's perspective using "I can" statements that help make lesson goals student-centered. The statements clearly communicate what students will be able to do after completing the lesson successfully.

Strategies for Creating

Overview:

Talking Drawings is a metacognitive strategy that demonstrates the impact of expanding definitions of school literacies to include visual and multimodal texts across the academic domains (Paquette, Fello, and Jalongo 2007; McConnell 1992). Using this strategy, students draw what they know about a topic, discuss their ideas with peers, participate in focused instruction, and revise their drawings to match their new understanding. There are several studies that advocate for drawing as a valued school communication mode, offering an additional way to demonstrate understanding, and as a more inclusive literacy practice (Brooks 2009; Hayik 2011; Zoss, Siegesmund, and Patisaul 2010; Whitin 2005). The benefits of the Talking Drawings Strategy include vocabulary development and effective correction of student misconceptions.

Purpose:

The Talking Drawings Strategy is a structured way to include drawing in classroom instructional practice. It creates an opportunity for students to draw what they know about a content-area topic and then incorporate new learning with prior knowledge. The writing component adds an additional layer of reflection as students describe the differences in their two drawings, noting new information.

Essential Question:

How does drawing pictures of prior and revised content knowledge support students' disciplinary and literacy learning as well as their ability to reflect on their new understanding?

Quick Ideas by Grade Level:

Grades K–1: Using Talking Drawings, students research other topics including the Statue of Liberty or other American symbols, characters from folklore, American legends, such as Pocahontas and Benjamin Franklin, and settings from long ago.

Grades 2–3: Use this strategy to study other topics including additional community workers, such as police officers, mail carriers, and judges, and people who made a difference, including Abraham Lincoln, Albert Einstein, and George Washington Carver.

Johnny Appleseed

Objectives

I can draw two pictures to show what I know before and after.

Materials

Provide each student with a two-section foldable or the Talking Drawings Activity Sheet on page 202 in Appendix B and in the Digital Resources. Students will also need drawing tools, such as pencils, colored pencils, and markers. Choose two to three texts to read aloud or video clips that are descriptive and provide information that can be included in student drawings. The texts for this lesson came from *Who Was Johnny Appleseed?* by Joan Holub and *Johnny Appleseed* by Jane Yolen.

Time

approximately 20 minutes

I DO

1. Whether being used to launch a unit or topic, or to revisit or build upon previously taught concepts, Talking Drawings should begin with a conversation.

2. Lead a discussion on the topic to activate prior knowledge. Ask, "What do you remember about Johnny Appleseed?"

3. Have students close their eyes and visualize Johnny Appleseed. Guide mental imaging based on all they have learned so far. Say, "Think about what Johnny Appleseed looks like. Where do you picture him?"

WE DO

1. After 30 seconds of thinking and visualizing, have students draw what they saw in their mind.

2. Say, "Now, open your eyes and in the first box, draw what you saw. Remember, this isn't art class, and you're not getting a grade on how well you draw Johnny Appleseed.

But it is important to pay attention to details when you make your picture. Try to make it look like the picture you had in your head."

3. Have students spend no more than five minutes sketching Johnny Appleseed in the first box.

YOU DO TOGETHER

1. After students complete their drawing, have them put their pencils down or away in their desks because the next two steps require active listening without sketching. Assure students that they will have another chance to draw in a few minutes.

2. Have students talk briefly with one another about their images, describing details and sharing ideas.

3. Conduct a read-aloud, shared reading, or viewing that provides additional information about Johnny Appleseed. Any texts provided at this step must be descriptive, with information that can be added to the drawings.

   • **Note:** Although this step is listed in the You Do Together section, it is best accomplished as a teacher-directed but collaborative part of the lesson, repeating the We Do section.

YOU DO ALONE

1. Have students draw a new picture of Johnny Appleseed for no more than five minutes in the second box of the Activity Sheets. Say, "Remember to include any new details or information you learned from our read-aloud."

2. Remind students to keep their markings in the second box and not to revise their initial images created in the first box.

3. After students have completed their second drawings, have them reflect on the differences between the two pictures. Have students circle or highlight the new information in the second pictures.

Differentiation for English Learners

- Have students label their images after each drawing.
- Provide additional visual support through photographs, drawings, or videos during the instruction section of the lesson (between the first and second drawings).

Writing for Transfer

Have students write captions for each image. Then, have them write about the differences between each drawing. Sentence frames provide additional support for young writers who are learning to write captions.

"In my first picture, _____ .

In my second picture, _____ .

My pictures are different because _____ ."

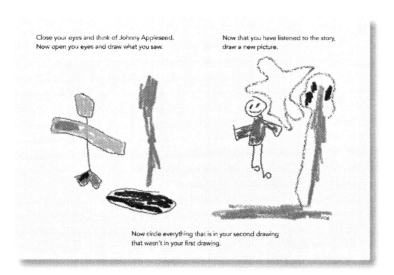

student work sample

Firefighters

Objectives

I can draw two pictures to show what I know before and after instruction. I can describe the differences in my pictures to identify new learning.

Materials

Provide each student with a three-section foldable or Talking Drawings Activity Sheet on page 203 in Appendix B and in the Digital Resources. Students will also need drawing tools, such as pencils, colored pencils, and markers. Choose two to three texts to read aloud or video clips that are descriptive and provide information that can be included in student drawings. The texts for this lesson came from two Teacher Created Materials sources: *A Day in the Life of a Firefighter* by Diana Herweck (available in Spanish) and *Firefighters Then and Now* by Melissa A. Settle.

Time

approximately 30 minutes

I DO

1. Whether being used to launch a unit or topic, or to revisit or build upon previously taught concepts, Talking Drawings should begin with a conversation.

2. Lead a discussion on the topic to activate prior knowledge. Say, "I know you have been learning a lot about firefighters in class this week."

3. Have students close their eyes and visualize a firefighter. Encourage students to create mental pictures based on all they have learned so far.

4. Ask, "Where do you see your firefighter? Think about your firefighter's gear. What is your firefighter wearing?"

WE DO

1. After 30 seconds of thinking and visualizing, have students draw what they saw in their minds.

2. Say, "Now, open your eyes and in the first box, draw what you saw. Remember, this isn't art class and you're not getting a grade on how well you draw your firefighters.

But I do want you to pay attention to details when you make your picture. Try to make it look like the picture you had in your head."

3. Have students spend no more than five minutes sketching their firefighters in the first box.

YOU DO TOGETHER

1. After students complete their first drawing, have them put their pencils down or away in their desks because the next two steps require active listening without sketching. Assure students that they will have another chance to draw in a few minutes.

2. Have students talk briefly with their partners about their images, describing details and sharing ideas.

3. Conduct a read-aloud, shared reading,

or viewing that provides additional information about firefighters. Excerpting from multiple texts is an option, as long as the text provided at this step is descriptive, with information that can be added to the drawings.

- **Note:** Although this step is listed in the You Do Together section, it is best accomplished as a teacher-directed but collaborative part of the lesson, repeating the We Do section.

YOU DO ALONE

1. Have students draw new pictures of a firefighter in the second box of the Activity Sheet for no more than five minutes. Say, "Remember to include any new details or information you learned from our shared reading."

2. Remind students to keep their markings in the middle box and not to revise their initial images created in the first box.

3. The back of the Activity Sheet is for written reflection. Have students study their two drawings and find the new and additional information in their second image.

4. Say, "How are your two drawings different?" This is the metacognitive section because students become aware of new learning and describe the differences on the back of the Activity Sheet.

Differentiation for English Learners

- Foster discussion by providing language frames to hang or post in the classroom.

  In my first picture _____ .

  In my second picture _____ .

  My pictures are different because _____ .

- Have students caption or label images with peers in between each step to develop and confirm academic vocabulary relevant to the specific topic.

- Provide additional visual support through photographs, drawings, or videos during the instruction section of the lesson (between the first and second drawings).

Writing for Transfer

The final step of the Talking Drawings Strategy involves a strong metacognitive writing component that can be fully developed into a unique written text on the differences between student drawings called "What I Learned About Firefighters." In addition, the drawing in the second box may serve as a prewrite to launch instruction on the genre of information text and using a descriptive text structure.

A second grader reflects on new learning, that firefighters can be female.

Integrating Technology

- During the firefighter Talking Drawings lesson, shared reading of the texts may be completed electronically. Digital texts are helpful.

- Talking Drawings lessons are well suited to be presented in PowerPoint or Google Slides, enabling each step in the lesson to be separated.

Reflective Questions

1. How does drawing in the first box help students activate prior knowledge relevant for the social studies topic?

2. How does the written reflection complement the student drawings? How can this be applied to other educational contexts?

Overview:

Collaborative Text Information Maps (CTIM) were created after observing teachers using aspects of Guided Language Acquisition Design (GLAD) professional development activities. CTIM are visualizations of content knowledge, maps that show where key historical and biographical events occurred. Teachers create maps as students sit close by and observe for additional cognitive benefits. Once the basic map is set, students collaborate to depict key events from a written text or video, using absolute and relative locations on the map. Later students return to the map to revisit, revise, and review the information presented. Students make additions throughout a unit of study.

Purpose:

This strategy is very helpful for representing both imagined and real communities where geography plays an essential role. It is particularly useful for the development of academic language. Following the CTIM process creates an inclusive learning environment where everyone has an opportunity to contribute.

Essential Question:

How does mapping a historical, biographical, or community event provide opportunities for students to demonstrate understandings about relative and absolute locations?

Quick Ideas by Grade Level:

Grades K–1: The CTIM process can be implemented effectively with the following texts:

- *Johnny Appleseed: The Legend and the Truth* by Jane Yolen
- *My Visit to the Zoo* by Aliki
- *Postal Workers Then and Now* by Cathy Davis

Grades 2–3: Texts for these grade levels include the following:

- *Coral Reefs* by Gail Gibbons
- *Lost and Found Cat: The True Story of Kunkush's Incredible Journey* by Doug Kuntz and Amy Shrodes
- *Paper Son: Lee's Journey to America* by Helen Foster James and Virginia Shin-Mui Loh

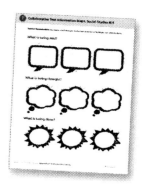

Mapping Market Street

Objectives

I can use relative location terms (*near/far*, *left/right*, and *behind/in front*) to map the events that happened in a community.

Materials

Choose a text that takes place in a community, real or imagined. Create a lightly drawn map of that place on large chart paper. Provide quotations or paraphrases from the text and images or symbols that represent action. This version uses three essential annotations that represent what the main character was thinking, saying, and doing to map the ideas and events in *Last Stop on Market Street* by Matt de la Peña. De la Peña is an author from California, and Market Street is a real place. The CTIM thought bubbles are located on pages 203–204 in Appendix B and in the Digital Resources.

What is being said?   **What is being thought?**   **What is being done?**

Time

two to three 20-minute lessons

I DO

1. **Read** aloud or do a shared reading of *Last Stop on Market Street*. This may be done during a different lesson or on a prior day.

2. Gather students close; proximity to the map is an important element of the CTIM Strategy. Trace over the map, which has been previously prepared and lightly illustrated in pencil.

3. As you draw the map, retell the information in the original text. Say, "We know CJ's story starts here at the church on Market Street. I'm going to show it's a church the way the illustrator, Christian Robinson, did and draw stained glass windows."

4. Be sure to use relative location words as you draw out the text information. Say, "Near the church was the bus stop. At the end of the street, very far to the right, was the last stop and the soup kitchen."

WE DO

1. **Revisit** the text interactively with students. This section can be taught later in the day or as another lesson. Add color to the chart in advance or during this section of the lesson (optional).

2. Distribute the talk, text, and action annotation bubbles to students. This is a great place for differentiation, as annotations can be specifically designed to meet a range of student needs because they contain images, symbols, and words.

3. Direct students to review their annotations and ask any questions about what is represented on their card.

4. Retell the events again. This time, students demonstrate active listening. Have each student come to the map and affix their annotations as they hear their event represented.

5. Have students use relative locations to describe where they are attaching their annotation. An example might be, "The bus stop is close to the church."

YOU DO TOGETHER

1. **Review** the map. This section should be done immediately after the retelling.

2. Place students in pairs to use the CTIM to practice retelling using relative locations. These terms may be listed on an illustrated anchor chart hung in the classroom for reference.

3. Have student pairs check the accuracy of the retelling and note any changes that may be needed. "Are all the represented events labeled on the correct places on the map of Market Street?"

CTIM Strategy
Read, Revisit,
Review, Revise

YOU DO ALONE

1. **Revise** the map, adding more information from the text.

2. Guide individual students create an additional talk, thought, or action annotation bubble to add to the CTIM as needed. Say, "What else happened on Market Street that we can add to our map?"

3. Have students use words, illustrations, and symbols to create map additions. Students can choose the type of annotation bubble, or you may differentiate by distributing them to each student.

4. This individual work may be an option for specific students who need additional academic challenges.

Differentiation for English Learners

- Assign students teacher-created quotes, paraphrases, illustrations, or symbols that represent the events in the text to place on the map in a small group.

- Have students use an oral retelling protocol that uses relative location academic vocabulary.

- Provide copies of the original book to guide their retelling of events as they review the map together.

Writing for Transfer

- Young writers can identify two events on the CTIM and describe them using relative locations.

- Sentence frames provide additional support as well as the anchor chart listing and illustrating relative locations.

    The _____ is near the _____ .

    The _____ is very far from the _____ .

    The _____ is to the right of the _____ .

Mapping George Washington Carver's Life

Objectives

I can draw a simple map that uses cardinal directions. I can describe locations to tell about a historical figure in a spatial context.

Materials

This version of the Collaborative Text Information Map (CTIM) begins with a map grid on a large chart. The relevant U.S. states (not the whole country) are drawn over the grid. In this example lesson on the life of George Washington Carver, the map includes Iowa, Kansas, Missouri, and Alabama. Provide text excerpts, illustrations, and/or symbols that represent the key events to be affixed to the corresponding spots on the map. Collaborative Text Information Maps are located on page 205 in Appendix B and in the Digital Resources. This Activity Sheet may be just the grid (for a Draw-Along) or may already have the relevant states indicated.

Three texts were included at different places in the lesson:

* *A Weed Is a Flower: The Life of George Washington Carver* by Aliki
* *Fantastic Kids: George Washington Carver* by Michelle Jovin
* *George Washington Carver: Planting Ideas* by Jennifer Kroll

Time

approximately 30–40 minutes

Note: This version was completed with a small group of emergent bilinguals. With additional excerpts and a larger chart, it could also be taught in a whole-group setting.

I DO

1. **Read** aloud or do a shared reading of one of the above texts. This may be done during a different lesson or on a prior day.

2. Gather students close because proximity to the map is an important element of the CTIM Strategy. Display a United States map, and show where George Washington Carver spent his life.

3. Conduct a Draw-Along or simply trace over the four key states. Label each state, and remind students that these are the important places in Carver's life.

4. Be sure to use relative location words as you draw out the basic map. Use cardinal directions as well. Say, "We see that Iowa is directly north of Missouri."

5. **Revisit** the basic map. Read the list of five key events in Carver's life that will be mapped. Model how to use the grid to find absolute locations on the map.

WE DO

1. As the large map is being built, have students complete their individual Activity Sheets, cutting and pasting each event onto the appropriate place on their maps.

2. At age 10 or 11, George Washington Carver left home to find a school because none of the nearby schools would take black children.

Draw-Along Strategy

The Draw–Along Strategy is a type of directed or guided drawing activity where students follow the teacher in very small step–by–step illustrations.

3. Say, "He walks 8 miles to Neosho, Missouri, to find a school that would accept him. That is a long walk, but it will show up nearby on our map. In fact, it is also at D5 just south of Diamond. Who will help us understand why it is placed on the map that way?"

YOU DO TOGETHER

1. Place students in pairs to find the next event on the map. They can demonstrate understanding by marking the place with their fingers before they glue the event onto the map.

2. Have them continue to work together to locate the other key events on their maps.

3. **Review** the map to reinforce skills. Say, "With your partner, find the event that is the furthest north on the map. Work together to find what event is at C4."

4. Have student pairs create a question about the map to share with the whole class.

YOU DO ALONE

1. Have individual students locate the last event on their maps at Tuskegee, Alabama. This event is farthest south and quite a distance from the others.

2. Check for understanding as individuals affix the event "George becomes a professor at the famous Tuskegee Institute in Tuskegee, Alabama," to their maps.

3. **Review** the available texts, and identify a sixth event that can be added to **revise** their map. The event must take place in one of the states identified as the most important to Carver's life (optional).

4. Have individual students use the map for an oral retelling of the key events in Carver's life.

Differentiation for English Learners

- Assign students teacher-created quotes, paraphrases, illustrations, or symbols that represent the events in the text to place on the map.

- Have students work in pairs to find the right place to contribute to the map.

- Provide copies of the original book to guide their retelling of events as they review the map together.

Writing for Transfer

Students use their CTIM to develop a prewrite about Carver. They return to the texts to find additional facts or events that occurred at each of the marked locations. This graphic then guides students as they write informative/explanatory (biographical) texts about Carver in which they introduce a topic, use the key facts and events identified on the map, and provide a concluding statement.

Integrating Technology

Google has many mapping tools with so many options for creating maps and graphing information on existing maps. These two resources help students visualize locations from different perspectives. My Maps is by far the most flexible and useful tool for visualizing location. Students can create maps with embedded links that take viewers to other resources and locations.

- **www.google.com/streetview/**
- **www.google.com/earth/**
- **www.google.com/mymaps/**

There are also many resources for free printable maps:

- **ontheworldmap.com/**
- **www.waterproofpaper.com/ printable-maps/**

Reflective Questions

1. What do the relative locations on maps tell the reader about the ways events connect?

2. What is the difference in comprehending locations from reading the text or visualizing their places on the CTIM?

Overview:

Storyboards are graphic organizers that visually sequence a narrative text and work as scaffolds for young writers as they plan their narratives. Storyboards can also be used to recount information after reading. When used to provide support this way, the strategy focuses on organizing text by chronology and guides students as they remember key details from narrative texts. Storyboards can take many approaches, making it an easy tool for differentiating in the classroom.

Purpose:

Students use illustrations, paraphrases, direct quotes, or any combination to express their understanding of the temporal order of events. Thus, Storyboards are useful for promoting the interconnectedness of all the language arts as students use both receptive and productive literacy modes.

Essential Question:

How can I visualize the chronology of key events in the narrative?

Quick Ideas by Grade Level:

Grades K–1: Students create three-box storyboards indicating beginning, middle, and end of the story. Before approaching narrative texts, students use a Storyboard to tell about their school day. "What is the first thing you do when you get to school? What happens next?" Illustrate the key events and use sequencing signal words to describe each box in the Storyboard.

Grades 2–3: Storyboards can be created to support science and social studies standards. For example, Storyboards can illustrate how a plant grows or depict the changes in the American flag over time.

All grades: Students across grade levels will benefit from creating an anchor chart from these mini lessons to highlight sequencing signal words. Anchor charts are best created along with students, using shared or interactive writing for engagement and to support skill transfer.

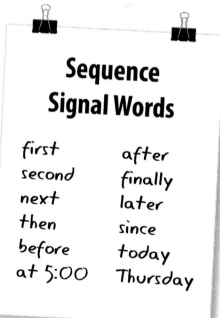

Sequence Signal Words

first	after
second	finally
next	later
then	since
before	today
at 5:00	Thursday

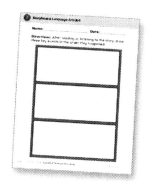

Storyboarding Aesop's Fables

Objectives

I can draw, dictate, or write to recount two or more events. I can include some details to tell about what happened.

Materials

Display three to six large images representing key story events from one of Aesop's fables as well as a large chart of the Storyboard. Provide plain white paper or one to two copies of the Storyboard Activity Sheet located on page 206 in Appendix B and in the Digital Resources, pencils, pens, markers, crayons, and other drawing tools for each student. For this example lesson, Aesop's "The Lion and the Mouse" is used.

Time

approximately 30 minutes

Cover Clues

Students use magnifying glasses and look closely at the cover image(s) for clues about what the text will be about. This is an especially useful strategy when widely retold stories, such as Aesop's fables, are available with different covers.

I DO

1. Share the cover of the fable, and help students look for cover clues they can use to make predictions about the text. Say, "When we read 'The Lion and the Mouse,' one of Aesop's fables, I want you to listen carefully to the sequence or order of the story."

2. Conduct an interactive read-aloud, pausing to clarify vocabulary and check the accuracy of predictions.

3. Display and describe each of the three images on the whiteboard or in a pocket chart. Model organizing the pictures in sequential order, indicating their place on the large Storyboard template with signal words.

4. Say, "I always start by looking for the event that happened first. In the beginning, Lion is asleep, and Mouse ran up onto him, and that's what this picture shows, so I will put it in the first box."

5. After modeling with the first key event on the Storyboard, look for the last event. Find the image that shows that even small Mouse was able to help Lion.

WE DO

1. As a class, review the beginning, middle, and end of the story. Use signal words, such as *next*, *then*, and *after*, as the pictures are placed on the large Storyboard template.

2. Share another fable with the same objective. Say, "Now, we are going to read 'City Mouse-Country Mouse' and once again look and listen for sequencing of key events in the story."

3. After reading the story, display a new large Storyboard template. Instead of placing existing images in the chart, draw an image that represents what happened in the beginning of the story: the City Mouse visits his cousin in the country. Use simple line drawings to communicate this idea and label the image "First."

4. Guide students to create their own drawings in the first box of the Storyboard Activity Sheets, reminding them that the purpose of their drawings is to show their thinking and not to look exactly like the picture in the book.

YOU DO TOGETHER

1. Have students discuss what they might draw in the last box of the Storyboard. "What could you draw that would show how the fable ends?"

2. Students may work together, but each student should draw their own images on their Storyboard Activity Sheets.

3. Have students discuss and plan the remaining events. Return to the first drawing. Ask, "What happens next? How can we use drawings to show those key story events?"

YOU DO ALONE

1. After discussing ideas with peers, have students illustrate in the remaining box on their Storyboards until they are complete.

2. Students may label each box with sequence signal words, such as *first, then, next,* etc.

3. Individual work can be used to monitor student progress toward understanding sequence.

Differentiation for English Learners

- Conduct a shared reading to guide students to connect the words to the visuals in the text.
- Have students work in small groups to create group Storyboards.
- Create a set of images excerpted from the text for students to organize before creating their own.

Writing for Transfer

- Students label each box on their Storyboards with a sequence signal word. An anchor chart is a good resource.
- Students tell the story in their Storyboards to their partner or tablemate. As they tell the story, they use at least five signal words. Partners listen closely and tally signal word usage.
- Students write using sentence frames.

  "First, _____ and then _____ . Finally, _____ ."

example of first-grade emergent bilingual Storyboard for "City Mouse-Country Mouse"

Storyboarding Basquiat

Objectives

I can tell about a sequence of events, using words to signal order. I can include details to describe actions, thoughts, and feelings.

Materials

Display a copy of Jean-Michel Basquiat's *Self Portrait*, 1984 and a large version of the Storyboard Activity Sheet. Each student will need plain white paper or Storyboard Activity Sheet, pencils, pens, markers, crayons, and other drawing tools. The Activity Sheet is located on page 207 in Appendix B and in the Digital Resources. The portrait is available only in the Digital Resources. This lesson focuses on the life of Basquiat as told in the book *Radiant Child* by Javaka Steptoe.

Time

approximately 30 minutes

I DO

1. Project Basquiat's *Self Portrait*, 1984, to introduce the artist. "Today, we are going to be reading about and recalling details about the life of the artist Jean-Michel Basquiat."

2. Use Character Clusters (page 55) or VTS (page 39) to lead a discussion about the image. It is important to build background knowledge before beginning to read because both the visual and written text are complex in *Radiant Child*.

3. Say, "The name of the book we are going to read is *Radiant Child*, and it is written and illustrated by Javaka Steptoe. *Radiant* may be a new word for you, but Steptoe has given us a visual clue about what it might mean."

4. Direct students to the uppercase *R* in *Radiant*, and lead a discussion clarifying the meaning of *radiant* as "giving off light or shining." Ask, "Why would Steptoe call Basquiat *radiant*?"

5. Conduct an interactive read-aloud, pausing to clarify vocabulary (*dwells, enchanted*) and figurative language ("a storm of papers"). Have students listen carefully to identify the key details and the sequence or order of the events in Basquiat's life.

WE DO

1. After reading, guide students to create a bulleted list of the key events in Basquiat's life. The list may include paraphrases, direct quotes, illustrations, or a combination of these approaches.

2. Basquiat uses several visual motifs (recurring ideas) in his paintings, including crowns, eyes, and cars. These may be added to the list of paraphrases to help students organize their thinking.

3. Best practices for Storyboards include beginning with the first illustration and then moving to the last illustration. Guide students to complete the illustrations on the Storyboards for the first box.

4. Place a check mark next to the life event on the list to model the connection between the Storyboard and the list of paraphrased events.

Radiant Child

Grows up in Brooklyn
As a boy he is a serious artist
He draws with his mama
He visits museums
He listens to jazz
He is in a car accident
He moves to New York City
People notice his graffiti
He becomes a famous artist!

5. Repeat the process for the last box.
   - **Note:** Third graders considered combining museum and jazz into one bullet.

YOU DO TOGETHER

1. Place students in pairs to narrow the list down to six key events that will complete the Storyboard. Students discuss why each incident may be considered a key event and not just something that happened.

2. Students may not come to a consensus about which are the most important or key events, but talking with their partners will help validate and elaborate their perspectives. "Why do you think this is a key event?"

YOU DO ALONE

1. Have individual students illustrate the remaining four events in the boxes on the activity sheet to complete the Storyboard.

2. Direct students to label each box with sequence signal words from page 123.

3. Individual work can be used to monitor student progress toward understanding sequence.

Differentiation for English Learners

- Create a set of images excerpted from the text for students to organize before creating their own.

- Have students work in small groups to create group Storyboards.

- Conduct a shared reading to help students connect the words to the visuals in the text.

Writing for Transfer

- After students list signal words for each of the boxes, they use the Storyboard as a prewrite activity to inform a draft. Students write to recall the events of Basquiat's life in the order in which they occur.

- Students research and write about the life of Javaka Steptoe, the author and illustrator of this book. Additional information can be found at **javaka.com**, including a tab with biographical information.

- Students create their own self-portraits in the style of Basquiat (messy and beautiful) and write their own stories.

Storyboard example

Storyboard
Wrap Up

Integrating Technology

There are many free and low-cost host sites and applications to support students of all ages as they create storyboards.

- **Storyboard That**
  www.storyboardthat.com/

- **Make Beliefs Comics**
  www.makebeliefscomix.com/

- **Storybird**
  storybird.com/

- **30 Hands Learning**
  30hands.com/

- **Pixton**
  www.pixton.com/

Reflective Questions

1. How does creating visual storyboards of key text events help recount and retell the story?

2. What role do size, color, and compositional placement have in communicating understanding?

Overview:

Understanding plot includes identifying many additional literacy features, such as key events, sequence, and causal relationships. Excitement Graphs visually depict the dramatic structure of text and, in this way, provide support for young learners as they bring all this rich information together to understand plot.

The earliest depictions of plot are attributed to Freytag's Pyramid, which visualizes a classic tragedy into five components (introduction, rising action, climax, falling action, and denouement). However, contemporary notions of visualizing plot are attributed to Kurt Vonnegut, who identified six story shapes—graphs that represent the most common story arcs.

Purpose:

Like the Storyboard Strategy, an Excitement Graph requires students to organize the key events sequentially. Indeed, the Excitement Graph is very often used as a follow-up strategy to a Storyboard in literacy and across academic domains. However, in addition to sequencing, students rank each event by how exciting, interesting, or important it is to the overall story. The resulting graph outlines the story plot. Excitement Graphs can also be used to visualize historical events.

Essential Question:

What does graphing the key story events by excitement, interest, or importance reveal about a narrative's plot?

Quick Ideas by Grade Level:

Grades K–1: Excitement Graphs can be completed with images excerpted from familiar stories and retellings of tales instead of student-created images. Create an Excitement Graph of a real-life experience in the classroom or school community using photographs of students to represent key events.

Grades 2–3:

* Photograph students' faces to represent the various levels of excitement along the vertical *y*-axis. What does bored look like? What does thrilled look like?

* Students explore Freytag's Pyramid and decide which of the five events represent each section of the pyramid.

* Small groups compare various texts on a theme and compare the shape of the resulting Excitement Graphs. For example, each group may graph a different Aesop's fable. Small groups of students can each graph a Cinderella story from a different part of the world.

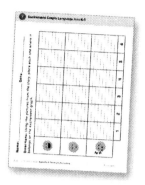

Plotting Aesop's Fables

Objectives

I can graph pictures of key story events by their level of excitement, interest, or importance. I can show I understand the plot.

Materials

Provide each student with three to six large images representing key story events, a student-completed Storyboard, and an Excitement Graph Activity Sheet located on page 208 in Appendix B and in the Digital Resources. Excitement Graph Activity Sheets are best if printed on ledger-sized 11" x 17" paper to accommodate the 2-inch boxes illustrated on an 8.5" x 11" letter-sized Storyboard. You will need a large Excitement Graph chart and markers for modeling. This lesson uses the fable from the Storyboard lesson.

Time

approximately 20–30 minutes

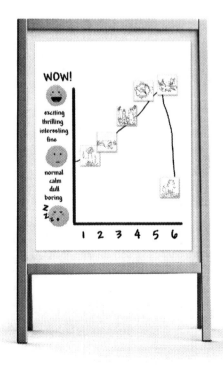

I DO

1. Return to the same images used to create the Storyboard of "The Lion and the Mouse" in the previous lesson. Say, "Now, we are going to rank each image by its level of excitement, interest, or importance. When we organize the key events in this way, we are learning about the plot of the story."

2. Introduce the graph. If students have not yet experienced a graph like this in mathematics, it will take some time to work through the components.

3. The numbers across the bottom horizontal line (*x*-axis) represent the key events. It may help to number the images on the Storyboard for students to see the connection.

4. Introduce the emoji along the left-hand vertical line (*y*-axis). Explain what each image represents (*dull, somewhat interesting, exciting*).

Excitement Graph
Language Arts **K–1** (cont.)

WE DO

1. Guide students to describe each emoji. Label with vocabulary words, such as *dull*, *thrilling*, etc. (optional).

2. Engage students in a discussion on where the first box from the Storyboard should be placed. Say, "Think about the Lion sleeping and the Mouse crawling on him. How exciting is this part? Is it boring? Is it thrilling?"

3. Continue the discussion, placing each of the Storyboard images in the Excitement Graph and noting the shape of the plot. Have students identify the most exciting key event.

4. Next, have students apply this experience to create their own Excitement Graphs from the Storyboards they created for the second fable, "City Mouse-Country Mouse." In addition to their Storyboards, each student has their own Excitement Graph activity sheet.

5. Prompt students as they decide the placement of the first box. Say, "In the beginning of our fable, the City Mouse goes to visit his cousin. Is this the most exciting part of the story? Is it the most uninteresting part of the story? Where should we place this on our graph?"

YOU DO TOGETHER

1. Have student pairs discuss and negotiate the placement of the second drawing from their Storyboards and compare the excitement in the second image to the first. Ask, "Is this key event more exciting than the first? How much more exciting? Why do you think so?"

2. However, student pairs do not have to agree and may have some variation in their rankings. After paired discussion, have students glue their second images to the place on their individual Excitement Graphs that best captures the level of excitement.

YOU DO ALONE

1. Now that students have practiced discussing and reasoning their perceptions of excitement, they are better equipped to complete the rest of the Excitement Graph on their own.

2. Have students carefully decide and place the remaining Storyboard boxes on their individual activity sheets, understanding that they must be ready to explain why they decided to put each key event in its place on the Excitement Graph.

51770—Get the Picture | **Strategies for Creating** 133

Differentiation for English Learners

- Have students create three- or four-box Excitement Graphs instead of using six images.

- Guide students to create their Excitement Graphs in small groups.

- Encourage discussion with a partner before individual placement of Storyboard boxes four, five, and six.

Writing for Transfer

Create a Gallery Walk of students' Excitement Graphs. As students move about the room, they notice how the plot shapes are the same and different, writing on sticky notes about the range of plot shapes. Students describe plot shapes; some are arcs and others may be more like a roller coaster ride. Students write about what the shape of the plot tells the reader about the story.

Gallery Walk

During a Gallery Walk, students view and think about multiple images displayed around the classroom. This is a great strategy for launching a unit of study. For example, imagine a classroom turned into a gallery of pictures of space or community landmarks.

Another way to use the Gallery Walk Strategy is to allow students to share their work with peers. Small groups or individual students rotate around the classroom, exploring and responding to peers' work.

Basquiat Excitement Graph

Objectives

I can graph illustrations of six key story events by their level of excitement, interest, or importance. I can show I understand the plot.

Materials

Provide each student with six images representing key story events from a completed Storyboard and an Excitement Graph Activity Sheet located on page 209 in Appendix B and in the Digital Resources. Excitement Graph Activity Sheets are best if printed on ledger-sized 11" x 17" paper to accommodate the 2-inch boxes illustrated on an 8.5" x 11" letter-sized Storyboard. You will need a large Excitement Graph chart and markers for modeling. This lesson uses an example from *Radiant Child* by Javaka Steptoe.

Time

approximately 20–30 minutes

I DO

1. Return to the same six images used to create the Storyboard of *Radiant Child* by Javaka Steptoe. Number each illustration in the sequence 1 to 6, then cut the images out of the Storyboard.

2. Say, "We've already learned how it is important to learn the sequence of the key story events. In today's lesson, we are going to build on that knowledge and rank each image by its level of excitement, interest, or importance. When we organize the key events in this way, we are learning about the plot of the story."

3. Introduce the graph. If students have not yet experienced a graph like this in mathematics, it will take some time to work through the components.

4. Say, "The numbers across the bottom horizontal line (*x*-axis) represent the key events. The vertical line on the left side of our graph (*y*-axis) will help us determine the excitement level of each key story event."

WE DO

1. Have students build a vertical linear array along the *y*-axis. Word relationships are an essential approach to building vocabulary knowledge and are an added benefit of the Excitement Graph.

2. Begin with words that represent opposite feelings of excitement. For example, mark *thrilling* at the top and *boring* at the bottom of the line.

3. Work with students, adding words to the array. Ask, "What is a word that is exciting but not as much as *thrilling*? Can you think of a word that is more exciting than *boring*?"

4. Engage students in a discussion about where the first box from the Storyboard should be placed. Say, "Think back to the beginning of Basquiat's life as told to us in *Radiant Child*. Many of us drew pictures that show him as an artist as a young boy. How exciting is that event? Is it the most exciting part of the story?"

YOU DO TOGETHER

1. Place students in pairs to discuss and negotiate the placement of the second drawing from their Storyboard, comparing the excitement level of the second image to the first one. Ask, "Is this key event more exciting than the first? How much more exciting? Why do you think so?"

2. However, student pairs do not have to agree and may have some variation in their ranking. Have students glue their second image to the place on their individual Excitement Graph that best captures the level of excitement.

3. Continue with paired discussion and individual placement for the third square. Remember to guide students to compare levels of excitement when making placement decisions.

TERMS TO KNOW

Linear Array

A linear array (Allen 2014; Nagy 1988) visually organizes vocabulary by the gradations between words in a category, best accomplished with any pair of opposites (*scream/whisper, hot/cold, large/small*). Begin with the obvious pair such as *large/small*. Have students find a word that represents something larger than large (*gigantic*) or smaller than small (*tiny*) or words smaller than large (*big*) and any nuance along the array. The strategy helps students develop word relationships including connections, distinctions, and shades of meaning.

YOU DO ALONE

1. Now that students have practiced discussing and reasoning their perceptions of excitement, they are better equipped to complete the rest of the Excitement Graph on their own.

2. Guide students to make comparisons to the first three events and then carefully decide and place Storyboard boxes four, five, and six on their individual activity sheets, understanding that they must be ready to explain why they decided to put each key event in its place on the Excitement Graph.

Differentiation for English Learners

- Model the Excitement Graph with images from a book before using student-made images.

- Have students create three- or four-box Excitement Graphs instead of using six images.

- Create Excitement Graphs in small groups with teacher guidance.

Writing for Transfer

Not only does the plot sequence key events but it helps us understand the causal relationships that reveal why things happen in the story. The Excitement Graph is an effective prewriting activity to guide students toward writing a biography. Students research important contemporary or historical characters and graph their key life events in an Excitement Graph to organize their writing.

Excitement Graph
Wrap Up

Integrating Technology

There are many free and low-cost graph-creating tools and apps online, including:

- **Kids' Zone: Learning with NCES**
  nces.ed.gov/nceskids/graphing/classic/

- **Canva's Online Graph Maker**
  www.canva.com/graphs/line-graphs/

- **Chart Tool**
  www.onlinecharttool.com/

- **Excel Easy**
  www.excel-easy.com/examples/line-chart.html

- **Google**
  www.draw.io

50%

Reflective Questions

1. What does the shape of the Excitement Graph tell the reader about the story plot?

2. What are the visual symbols and pictorial features that help illustrate key events?

Overview:

Listen to Me is a high-utility strategy that has been successfully implemented across curriculums and grade levels. Like many of the visual-based instructional strategies in this text, Listen to Me grew out of a museum experience. A docent at the Getty Museum in Los Angeles practiced this approach with a group of students paired in lines in front of *Wheatstacks, Snow Effect, Morning* (1891) by Claude Monet. One set of students had their backs to the painting and were drawing what their partners described.

Purpose:

This strategy provides a way for students to practice speaking and listening skills as they take turns describing and analyzing visually presented information and recording what their partner shares. It also requires students to create illustrations to show their geometric understanding described in grade-level standards.

Essential Question:

How can students confirm understanding of orally presented mathematical information through drawing two-dimensional shapes?

Quick Ideas by Grade Level:

Kindergarten: Students identify, name, and describe basic two-dimensional shapes, such as squares, triangles, circles, rectangles, and hexagons, presented in a variety of ways (e.g., with different sizes and orientations).

Grade 1: Students combine shapes, recognize them from different perspectives and orientations, describe their geometric attributes, and determine how they are alike and different.

Grade 2: Students describe and analyze shapes by examining their sides and angles. Students investigate, describe, and combine shapes to make other shapes.

Grade 3: Students describe, analyze, and compare properties of two-dimensional shapes. They compare and classify shapes by their sides and angles, and they connect these with definitions of shapes.

"A drawing is simply taking a line for a walk."
—Paul Klee (1879–1940)

Paul Klee was a Swiss-German painter who taught at the Bauhaus in the 1920s. His lectures are published in the Paul Klee Notebooks.

Drawing Shapes

Objectives

I can describe two-dimensional shapes by looking at their traits. I can show understanding by drawing two-dimensional shapes.

Materials

Create an anchor chart of basic shapes, such as rectangles, triangles, and squares, before the lesson or with the students. Gather five to ten shapes to display for students. Provide paper, pencils, and clipboards for students. This lesson is the Writing for Transfer assignment described on page 142. The Listen to Me Activity Sheet is located on page 210 in Appendix B and in the Digital Resources.

Time

approximately 10–20 minutes

Each turn takes about five minutes. Every lesson should include two or four turns, ensuring students have the opportunity to take on both roles of drawing and describing.

I DO

1. Start by building (or referring to) an anchor chart that highlights the shape possibilities. Draw, label, and describe each shape (rectangles, triangles, squares, etc.), activating prior knowledge and preparing for the lesson.

2. Stand with your back to the classroom screen. Tell students they are going to see a shape and they have to describe it so that you can draw it without looking.

3. Say, "When you describe the shape, you can talk about its sides, angles, or whether it is open or closed, but you cannot name the shape."

4. Project a rectangle. You can use a hand drawing or image on your computer or tablet.

WE DO

1. Have students take turns giving descriptions as you draw what they say.

2. Use nonexamples whenever possible. For example, if a student describes two long lines and two short lines, you may draw a quadrilateral that is not a rectangle or draw the long sides horizontally instead of vertically.

3. Next, you describe and students draw. Model the process again, this time with students drawing to your description of a triangle.

4. Be sure to include academic vocabulary in your description and emphasize defining attributes. This two-step modeling is important to reinforce the importance of precise descriptive language and the explicitness of geometric definitions.

YOU DO TOGETHER

1. Bring the students to the carpet closer to the screen. Have a row of students sit with their backs to the screen with partners who face the screen. Each pair has a clipboard, paper, and pencil for sketching.

2. Give students facing the illustration three to five minutes to describe the geometric shape without naming it. Students can describe lines, angles, etc. as modeled.

3. Following the initial drawing time, allow the drawing students to ask questions for one additional minute and to continue drawing (optional).

4. When time is up, have students look at the original drawing. Say, "How is your shape the same or different from the original drawing on the screen?"

5. Have students switch roles so they have the opportunity to draw and describe in every lesson.

YOU DO ALONE

1. Have students draw at least one more shape in each category. For example, if their partner describes a triangle, they draw a different type of triangle.

2. This builds categorical understandings and reinforces the defining attributes of each shape.

3. Individual drawings are also helpful for monitoring progress toward the lesson objectives.

Differentiation for English Learners

- Guide students to use oral language frames to describe the similarities and differences between their drawing and the shape as displayed.

  "My shape is the same because _____ . My shape is different because _____ ."

- Have students label the drawn images with defining attributes.

Writing for Transfer

Following the oral language and drawing components of the lesson, students write about their shapes, explicitly naming their defining attributes. Each shape has its own page that is compiled into a book. Some teachers use index cards and a binder ring so students have a readily available resource to reference.

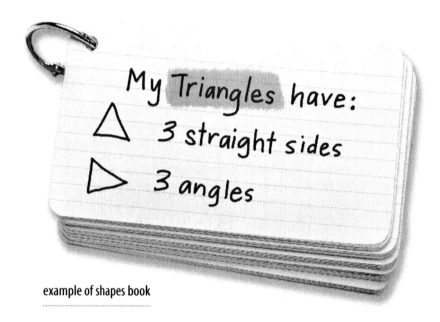

example of shapes book

Combining Shapes

Objectives

I can describe and compare properties of two-dimensional shapes using their defining traits. I can show understanding by drawing combinations of two-dimensional shapes.

Materials

Create an anchor chart of shapes before the lesson or with the students. Gather 10 basic shape drawings to display. Provide paper, pencils, and clipboards for students. For this lesson, the Listen to Me Activity Sheet is the Writing for Transfer assignment located on page 211 in Appendix B and in the Digital Resources.

Time

approximately 20–30 minutes

Each turn takes about five minutes. Every lesson should include four to six turns, ensuring students have more than one opportunity to take on both roles of drawing and describing.

right triangle	triangle with one right angle	
isosceles triangle	triangle with two equal sides	
scalene triangle	triangle with no equal sides or angles	
equilateral triangle	triangle with all equal sides	
trapezoid	a quadrilateral with one pair of parallel sides	
parallelogram	a quadrilateral with two pairs of parallel sides	
hexagon	a six-sided polygon	
octagon	an eight-sided polygon	

I DO

1. Display the painting *Municipal Jewel* by Paul Klee. This artist used combinations of shapes to express himself and his ideas. Have students read the image and identify all the shapes they see in the painting. Record a list.

2. Start by building an anchor chart that highlights the shapes under study and reinforces academic vocabulary. Draw, label, and describe each shape, activating prior knowledge and preparing for the lesson.

3. Stand with your back to the classroom screen. Tell students they are going to see a shape and they have to describe it so that you can draw it without looking.

4. Say, "When you describe the shape, you can talk about its sides, angles, or whether it is open or closed, but you cannot name the shape. Use academic vocabulary."

5. Project a rectangle. In this example lesson, a rectangle built of two squares is used to focus on combining shapes. Use a hand drawing or image on your computer or tablet.

WE DO

1. Have students take turns giving descriptions as you draw what they say.

2. Use nonexamples whenever possible. For example, if a student describes two long lines and two short lines, you may draw a quadrilateral that is not a rectangle, or you may draw the long sides horizontally instead of vertically.

3. Model the process again, this time with students drawing to your description of a triangle. Be sure to include academic vocabulary in your description and emphasize defining attributes.

4. This two-step modeling is important to reinforce the importance of precise descriptive language and the explicitness of geometric definitions. It sets the stage for the more complex drawings to follow.

YOU DO TOGETHER

1. Bring the students to the carpet closer to the screen. Have a row of students sit with their backs to the screen with partners who face the screen. Each pair has a clipboard, paper, and pencil for sketching.

2. Give students facing the illustration no more than five minutes to describe the geometric shapes without naming them. Students can describe lines, angles, etc. as modeled. Have them include relative locations in their description to create combinations of shapes.

3. Following the initial time, allow the drawing students to ask questions for one additional minute and to continue drawing (optional).

4. When time is up, have students look at the original drawing. Say, "How are your shapes

the same or different from the original drawing on the screen?"

5. Have students switch roles so they have the opportunity to draw and describe in every lesson.

Marva's Classroom Moment
The original plan for this lesson included students creating Listen to Me drawings that were as complex as some of Paul Klee's work. We found three or four shapes in a combination was the maximum amount that could be drawn by our third graders.

YOU DO ALONE

1. Have students draw at least one more combination of shapes that matches the original. For example, if their partner describes an isosceles triangle and a trapezoid, students draw another—but different—combination of an isosceles triangle and trapezoid.

2. This builds categorical understandings and reinforces the defining attributes of each shape. Individual drawings are also helpful for monitoring progress toward the lesson objectives.

Differentiation for English Learners

- Consider who might benefit most from listening before speaking or the reverse when pairing students.

- Guide students to use oral language frames to describe the similarities and differences between their drawings and the shape as displayed.

    "My shapes are the same because _____ . My shapes are different because _____ ."

- Provide students an opportunity to revise their drawings. Ask, "What can you do to make it better match the combination of shapes in the original drawing?"

Writing for Transfer

Following the oral language and drawing components of the lesson, have students write about their shapes. Students draw a page for each shape listed on the anchor chart. Each shape has its own page and may be compiled into a book. Some teachers use index cards and a binder ring, so students have a readily available resource to reference. See Appendix B on page 211.

Integrating Technology

This lesson features drawings created on the free Paper App for iPad: **www.fiftythree.com /paper**. Drawings, rather than clip art, were used intentionally so students could see real-life variations reflected in their own drawings. Listen to Me drawings were projected directly from an iPad.

Other free drawing applications include:

- **Sketchpad**
  sketch.io/sketchpad/
- **Doodle Buddy**
  itunes.apple.com/au/app/doodle-buddy
  -paint-draw-scribble/id313232441
- **Draw It!**
  itunes.apple.com/au/app/draw-free-for
  -ipad/id366755447

Reflective Questions

1. What role does drawing have on geometrical understanding?

2. How does drawing to oral-language descriptions impact relevant academic vocabulary?

Overview:

Visual Measurement helps students acquire knowledge about determining the size of things. This strategy creates interest and encourages thinking about results by using nonstandard units of measures with visuals for application. Prior to the instruction of the targeted math element, students are presented with a series of complex images for close reading and vocabulary appropriate for measurement. They are encouraged to produce estimates of measurement and then provide evidence for justification. In addition, visual measurement provides a platform for students to create their own designs.

Purpose:

Visual Measurement provides a way for students to build background knowledge and vocabulary of measurement by closely examining images. Students have the opportunity to apply their knowledge of measurement to the selected image and produce a design of their own using the same rules for measurement. This strategy requires students to discuss attributes of the images, activate background knowledge, apply vocabulary, participate in an oral language experience, and identify a purpose for reading the image.

Essential Question:

How can students use images to estimate and measure size?

Quick Ideas by Grade Level:

Kindergarten: Students stand next to their partners and compare heights.

Grades 1–3: After discussing nonstandard measures, students identify sizes of objects in the classroom and predict estimates of measurement. Students write about their findings and use academic language in their justifications.

Visual Measurement
Mathematics K–1

Nonstandard Measurement

Objectives

I can draw and write to identify the height and width in visual texts.

Materials

Gather at least 10 visual images from electronic sources and linking plastic cubes for nonstandard measurement. Student drawings may also be used for visual analysis. In this example lesson, an image of a colonial house is used. The Visual Measurement Activity Sheet is located on page 212 in Appendix B and in the Digital Resources. The image is in the Digital Resources.

Time

approximately 30 minutes

I DO

1. Model the strategy with a focus on the design of the colonial house. Using a pointer or finger, read the image top to bottom and left to right, noting how much can be learned about the design from closely reading the photograph.

2. Use the Think-Aloud Strategy, and provide evidence to support a claim. Say, "From looking at this photograph, I can see the front of a house, a roof, a door, and windows."

3. As you read the image, label these words on the side of the photograph. It is important for the students to see the image in the photograph.

4. Say, "There is a way to understand how tall this house is in this photograph. I am going to use these cubes as counters to determine how tall and wide the house is in this photograph. I notice that the wall is four cubes tall." Continue to measure the width of the house, the roof, and the bottom of the house.

5. Say, "Now, I am going to draw my own house using cubes for measurement." Proceed by drawing using cubes for nonstandard measurement and using academic language descriptors. Say, "My roof is two cubes tall and four cubes wide."

WE DO

1. As a class, work together by closely reading the drawing and continue the discussion about measurement, using cubes as a nonstandard measure to determine the width and height of the house.

2. Record (based on student discussion) the measurements discussed by the class on the board.

3. Have students cite evidence in the discussion. Ask, "How do you know the house has a wall three blocks tall?"

 Nancy's Classroom Moment

Encourage students to justify their responses.

Student 1: What can you do with cubes?

Student 2: Build something.

Nancy: I want to measure how tall the house is. (Places cubes on the house for measurement.)

Nancy: Do I need another block? Let's measure the blocks by counting.

Student 3: One, two, three, four.

Student 4: The house is four blocks tall.

YOU DO TOGETHER

1. Place students in small groups. Have them identify measurements in another photograph.

2. Have groups provide evidence in each photograph that supports the lesson objective.

YOU DO ALONE

1. Guide individual students to produce their own designs using blocks as their nonstandard measurements.

2. Have students record by writing numbers that support their measurements.

3. Independent work may serve as an assessment to monitor student progress toward the objective.

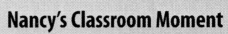 **Nancy's Classroom Moment**

This is a good opportunity to start a discussion about comparisons between images.

Nancy: Let's look at this student's house. Is it larger or smaller than my house? Is it the same or different?

Student 1: Different.

Nancy: Let's count how tall her house is.

Student 2: Her house is four blocks tall. It is smaller than your house.

Differentiation for English Learners

- Have students work with word strings to increase their vocabulary about size.

shorter	**taller**
smaller	**larger**
narrow	**wide**

- Foster discussion around evidence by providing language frames to hang or post in the classroom. "I measured the wall, and it is _____ blocks tall."

- Encourage oral language by having students take their designs home and explain to their parents or siblings how they measured and drew their designs.

- Create a class book with the student designs for a shared-reading lesson.

Writing for Transfer

Visual Measurement is the perfect platform for students to write or state a prediction about the math lesson. Have them measure objects in the classroom and on their desks.

"My book is _____ blocks tall."

If students cannot write, they can draw a picture by using their blocks as their nonstandard measure.

example of a kindergarten student's visual measurement for a house

Nonstandard Measurement

Objectives

I can use height, length, and width to describe and draw an image.

Materials

Provide at least 10 visual images from electronic sources and paper clips for nonstandard measurement. Student drawings may also be used for visual analysis. This example lesson uses an image of Tower Bridge located in the Digital Resources. The Visual Measurement Activity Sheet is located on page 213 in Appendix B and in the Digital Resources.

Time

approximately 30 minutes

I DO

1. Model the strategy with a focus on the design of the bridge. Using a pointer or finger, read the image top to bottom and left to right, noting how much can be learned about the design from closely reading the photograph.

2. Use the Think-Aloud Strategy to provide evidence to support a claim. Say, "From looking at this photograph, I can see that the bridge has two tall structures on each end in the shape of rectangles."

3. Say, "There is a way to understand how tall this bridge is in this photograph. I am going to use paper clips as counters to determine how tall and wide the bridge is in this photograph."

4. Proceed by placing the paper clips along the sides of the bridge for measurement. Say, "I notice that the left wall is four paper clips tall." Continue across the width of the bridge.

5. Say, "I am going to now draw my own design (building or bridge) using paper clips for measurement." Proceed with your own demonstration drawing, using paper clips for nonstandard measurement.

WE DO

1. As a class, work together by closely reading the photograph and drawing, and continue the discussion about measurement using paper clips as a nonstandard measure to determine the width and height of the bridge.

2. Record the measurements discussed by the class using a document camera, if available, or on the board.

3. Have students cite evidence in the discussion. For example, ask, "How do you know the width of the bridge is five paper clips?"

YOU DO TOGETHER

1. Place students in small groups. Have them identify measurements in a different photograph.

2. Have groups provide evidence in each photograph that supports the lesson objective.

YOU DO ALONE

1. Guide individual students produce their own designs using paper clips as their nonstandard measurement.

2. Have students record by writing numbers that support their measurements.

3. Independent work may serve as an assessment to monitor student progress toward the objective.

4. Use this time as an opportunity for students to make connections to their STEM work. "Talk to your partner and explain the science, technology, engineering, and math involved in your design."

Nancy's Classroom Moment

Encourage students to work with their partners and compare their findings.
Nancy: Talk to your partner and share your measurements. Tell which measurements are alike.
Student 1: This is three clips long.
Student 2: We both have the same for the left tower.
Student 1: Most sides have two clips.

Student Resources: Math-Based Literature

Children's literature provides another opportunity for deeper understanding of measurement and can easily be incorporated into a math lesson. For example, *How Tall, How Short, How Faraway* by David A. Adler and *Millions to Measure* by David M. Schwartz reinforce the elements of measurement with captivating photography.

Differentiation for English Learners

- Allow time for students to work collaboratively using oral language to describe their measurements.

    "The width of this side is _____."

- Provide kinesthetic demonstrations to illustrate height and width using your arms.

- Encourage oral-language development through Modeled Talk (Herrell 1999), where student pairs share the steps they took to design their buildings and how they obtained the measurements.

Writing for Transfer

Visual Measurement is a platform for writing. Students can write a story that discusses the origin of their building and the measurements required for the design.

Use this time to expand the vocabulary of the discipline. Students can respond to the following writing prompts:

- How would an architect look at and describe this drawing?

- What features are important for a biologist to consider?

- Describe concerns that would be addressed by an environmentalist.

Integrating Technology

Grades K–1

- Working individually or with a partner, students can review length, width, and height using the **splashmath.com** app.

- Build the pattern 5 with virtual pattern blocks on interactive whiteboards at **nlvm.usu.edu**.

- Sheppardsoftware.com is a great tool to access primary math games for K–2 (counting 1 to 5 and 1 to 10).

Grades 2–3

Review and reinforcement of measurement can be found in a variety of activities using **www.sheppardsoftware.com**.

Reflective Questions

1. How does viewing the image support readers in analyzing size as it relates to measurement?

2. How does close reading of images support math content?

Overview:

Research has identified science as the academic domain in which teachers use graphical representations most often (Coleman, McTigue, and Smolkin 2011). This same study found that, by far, referencing these visuals in textbooks is the most used instructional practice. Teachers are utilizing graphic representations, but students are not being engaged with creating their own illustrations or other graphic representations. The Properties and Categories of Matter chart can be used for instruction across academic disciplines.

Purpose:

This visual-based strategy aims to bring balance to receptive and productive modes of visual communication by capitalizing on drawn and photographic expressions of understanding science concepts. Literacy requires students to use drawing along with dictation and writing to convey informative/explanatory understandings.

Essential Question:

How can students create visual categories of matter grouped by physical properties?

Quick Ideas by Grade Level:

Grades K–1: Categories can be created that sort by any observable properties. Students create charts based on color or shape. Students create categories of community workers in social studies.

Grades 2–3: Categories may help visually sort matter by state (solid, liquid, gas). Categories can illustrate the way matter interacts. What properties respond to magnetic forces?

Sorting by Shape and Color

Objectives

I can sort matter by observing its properties. I can draw additions to the given groups.

Materials

Gather an image bank of 15 to 20 images that represent a range of observable properties, including a variety of shapes and colors. Choose photographs and drawings to represent different visual genres. Each student will also need the Properties and Categories of Matter Activity Sheet, and a large chart version of this graphic is needed for the teacher. The Properties and Categories of Matter Activity Sheet is located on page 214 in Appendix B and in the Digital Resources.

Time

approximately 20 minutes

I DO

1. Display three or four images in the first row of a large three-column chart. Connect to the study of matter (everything that takes up space and has mass). See page 158 for an example.

2. Describe matter by its properties. Physical properties of matter are those things that can be seen and felt; they are observable.

3. Identify the first object, and describe and list its observable properties. Say, "This is an apple. It is round and red and shiny."

4. Using the image bank, find another picture that has one of the same properties, grouping matter by properties to make categories.

5. Say, "This egg is also round. Let's make this a category of round objects." Paste the egg into the second column, and circle the word *round* in the list next to the apple.

WE DO

1. Elicit ideas from students, and draw a round item (such as Earth or an orange) in the third column.

2. With the help of the students, name and list the properties of the second object, a tree. "The tree is tall and green and brown."

3. Invite a student or pair of students to the image bank to find an image of something with one of the same properties. Say, "The tea is also green. Let's make this a category of green objects." Paste the tea into the second column, and circle the word *green* in the list next to the tree.

YOU DO TOGETHER

1. Place students in small groups to generate ideas of objects they might draw that are green and fit the category. Then, each student draws something green in the third column on the activity sheet.

2. Have small groups list the properties of a third object, such as a cloud. "It is white and puffy."

YOU DO ALONE

1. Guide individual students choose a picture from the image bank that represents one of the properties of clouds. Have them glue the picture into the second column and create their own category by circling the word on the list.

2. Have students draw a third item that matches that property in the third column.

3. Independent work may serve as an assessment to monitor student progress toward the objective.

Differentiation for English Learners

- Limit the image bank to the number of images needed to fill the chart to make categorizing more explicit.

- To lower the affective filter for greater participation, have students use a larger image bank and glue in two objects that represent the property and help build a category.

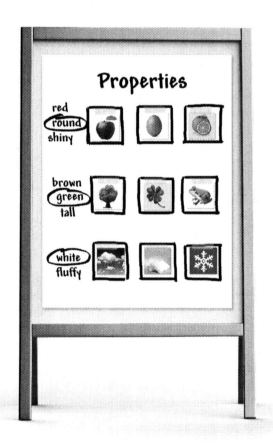

example of Properties Chart

Writing for Transfer

Students use their Properties and Categories of Matter chart to write brief informative/explanatory statements. They choose one object in each category to represent each property.

- The orange is round.
- The tree is green.
- The pillow is soft.

Creating Categories of Physical Properties

Objectives

I can compare and sort objects by observing their properties and traits.
I can draw and photograph additions to the given categories.

Materials

Gather an image bank of 15–20 visual texts that represent a range of observable properties, including a variety of shapes, colors, and textures for this lesson. Size is another category that can be visually assessed. Teachers can use size to quickly introduce the topic of properties or assign the concept as an activity for students to complete on their own. Students will also need the Properties and Categories of Matter Activity Sheets, and a large chart version of this graphic is needed for the teacher. The Properties and Categories of Matter Activity Sheet is located on page 215 in Appendix B and in the Digital Resources. This example lesson uses a tablet or smartphone to create photographs.

Time

approximately 30 minutes

I DO

1. Display three or four images in the first column of a large four-column version of the activity sheet on page 215. Connect to the study of matter (everything that takes up space and has mass).

2. Describe matter by its properties for students. Say, "Physical properties of matter are those things we can see and feel; they are observable."

3. The images chosen for this lesson represent different properties, including shape, color, and texture. Identify the first object, and describe and list its observable properties. "This is an apple. It is round and red and shiny." Place the apple on Image 1.

4. Look in the image bank, and find another picture that has one of the same properties. Say, "When we group matter by properties, we make categories. This egg is also round. Let's make this a category of round objects."

5. Model pasting the egg into the Image 2 column. Write the word *round* in the shape properties next to the apple.

WE DO

1. With the help of the students, name and list the properties of the second object, a tree. The tree is tall and green and brown.

2. Use the image bank to find an image of something with one of the same properties.

Say, "The tea is also green. Let's make this a category of green objects." Glue the tree on Image 1 in the second row. Paste the tea next to the tree, and write the word *green* in the color properties column.

YOU DO TOGETHER

1. Have student pairs list the properties of the third object, a chair, which is purple and soft. Glue the chair in Image 1 on the third row. Have them choose a picture from the image bank that represents one of the properties of the chair.

2. "The pillows are also soft. Let's make this a category of soft objects." Paste the pillows into the second column, and write the word *soft* in the texture properties column next to the chair.

3. Then, have student pairs take photographs (or make drawings) that match the properties in each category for the third column. For example, students must find something round in their classroom (or at their school) that can be photographed (or drawn) and added to the first row of their chart: the "round" property.

4. Say, "What are our three categories? We need to find objects in our classroom that can be added to each category."

YOU DO ALONE

1. Have students take one photograph per category using available technology. If possible, use a small printer to make stickers of each photo. If no cameras are available, students can draw.

2. In this lesson, each student created three pictures: one round object, one green object, and one soft object.

3. Have students review their charts and affix each property sticker into the correct category row to complete the chart.

4. Independent work may serve as an assessment to monitor student progress toward the objective.

Differentiation for English Learners

• Provide time for students to discuss what to draw or photograph with their peers.

• Limit the number of categories to one or two depending on their language acquisition.

Writing for Transfer

Using the information collected on their Properties and Categories of Matter charts, students write brief informative/explanatory books in which they name a topic, supply some facts about the topic, and provide some sense of closure.

Marva's Classroom Moment

Gil is a second-grade emergent bilingual with less than a year of formal English instruction. "I know there is a tree here (pointing to activity sheet), but would it be different to just photograph the palms and not the tree part? Wait! I have a better idea. What color are your eyes, Dr. Marva?"

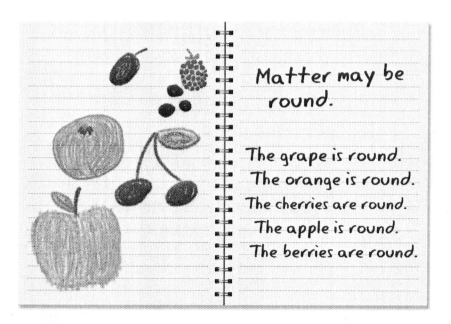

example of an explanatory book

Integrating Technology

Tablet and smartphone technology connected to a Bluetooth printer is recommended for completing this strategy. However, teachers may also choose to use inexpensive digital cameras. If a camera is used, you will need the appropriate adapter to read the memory card when it is removed from the camera. Attach the card reader to a computer or tablet, and print as described above.

Reflective Questions

1. How does creating charts complement and expand reading categorical information in the disciplines of science and literacy?

2. What advantages does using existing images provide to students? How might offering different ways to create images for the chart (drawing and photography) offer additional support for students learning literacy and science?

Overview:

Another way to introduce classification is through the use of pictures. Classify This! helps students determine how to categorize pictures to represent data. Prior to the instruction of the targeted science objective, students are presented with a series of complex images for close reading and vocabulary appropriate for classification. They are encouraged to determine criteria for grouping and then provide evidence for justification. Students learn attributes, rules, or criteria that determine categories, which results in classification. Classify This! provides a platform for students to create their own designs.

Purpose:

This strategy provides the opportunity for students to discuss the images, apply vocabulary, participate in an oral language experience, and identify a purpose for reading the image. Students apply their knowledge of classification for the selected topic and chosen images, produce a design of their own, and provide criteria for their classifications.

Essential Question:

How can using images to understand classification support students' disciplinary and literacy learning?

Quick Ideas by Grade Level:

Grades K–1: Students identify objects in the classroom and sort them into groups. Students classify survival needs for plants and animals.

Grades 2–3: Interpret and classify fossils and their environments, including marine fossils, plant fossils, and fossils of extinct organisms.

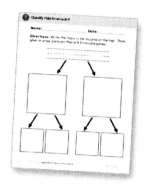

Animal Habitats

Objectives

I can break down images and sort into groups.

Materials

Provide 10 to 15 visual images of animals and their habitats. Make enough copies for students to glue on their Activity Sheets and provide glue sticks. Alternatively, students can draw on their Activity Sheets using colored pencils or markers. In addition, they will need the Classify This! Activity Sheet located on page 216 in Appendix B and in the Digital Resources.

Time

approximately 30 minutes

Pockets charts are an effective tool to use when demonstrating levels of classification.

I DO

1. Using picture cards in a pocket chart, model the strategy with a focus on images of animals and their habitats.

2. Reading the photographs say, "There is a way to understand how to group these photographs and understand their differences. First, let's see what they have in common. This will help me group the images. I notice that there are three animals and three animal habitats. Habitats are places where animals live."

3. Say, "I am going to place the photos of animals in this row. Now, I am going to locate the habitat where each animal lives and place it directly below the animal." Continue moving images into a hierarchy on the pocket chart.

4. Now, model the same process by gluing images down on the hierarchy chart by classification. Use language for classification as you draw the image. Say, "This is a _____ and lives in _____ ."

WE DO

1. As a class, work together to closely read the photographs and continue the discussion about animal classification.

2. Determine the groupings of animals and their habitats.

3. Record (based on student discussion) the classifications discussed by the class.

4. Have students cite evidence in the discussion. "Why did you group the images that way?"

YOU DO TOGETHER

1. Place students in small groups to continue to identify additional ways to group the photographs.

2. Have each group provide evidence from each photograph that supports the lesson objective.

YOU DO ALONE

1. Have individual students produce their own design of animal classification by gluing pictures to their Activity Sheets. Then, ask them to explain their justification with their table groups with oral or written language.

2. Independent work may serve as an assessment to monitor student progress toward the objective.

Student Resources: Science-Based Literature

Children's literature provides another opportunity for deeper understanding of classification and can easily be incorporated into a math lesson. For example, *A House Is a House for Me* by Mary Ann Hoberman provides an abundance of living and nonliving examples with their habitats.

Differentiation for English Learners

- Have students work with objects in the classroom in order to understand classification before moving to pictures.

- Encourage oral language by having students take their activity sheets home and work with parents or siblings by classifying and drawing objects around the home.

- Create a class book with the student designs for a review lesson on classification.

Writing for Transfer

- Classify This! is the perfect platform for students to write a prediction about the science lesson.

  "Our science lesson will be about _____ ."

- Look around the classroom and classify objects. Write a sentence with the classification. "My desk is a type of furniture."

- Build a science word wall to encourage students to use content-area vocabulary in their writing.

Animal Habitats

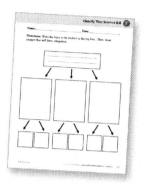

Objectives

I can show understanding of pictures of a topic. I can draw images that fit a visual representation of groupings.

Materials

Provide 10 to 15 images of animals and drawing tools such as pencils, colored pencils, or markers. Students will also need copies of the Classify This! Activity Sheet located on page 217 in Appendix B and in the Digital Resources.

Time

approximately 30 minutes

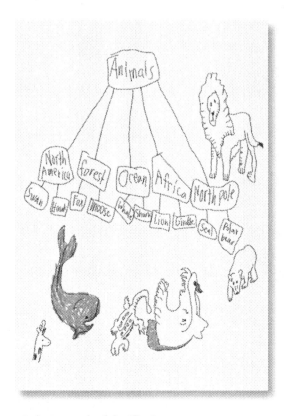

student example of classification

I DO

1. Using picture cards in a pocket chart, model the strategy with a focus on images of animals and their habitats.

2. Use the Think-Aloud Strategy, and provide evidence to support any claims. Say, "From looking at these photographs, I can see that some animals make good house pets, and others live in the wilderness."

3. Say, "I am going to categorize these images and determine criteria for their classifications." Demonstrate by moving the photographs into two levels. Write the criteria as you organize the images.

4. Say, "I have organized these images into two classifications. These images are house pets and live in the house or backyard. These images are wild animals that live in the forest, bush, or desert."

5. After establishing criteria, examine a few more images and begin to draw the classifications.

WE DO

1. Guide students to read the remaining photographs and contribute to the discussion about classification.

2. As a class, work together to classify pictures according to set criteria.

3. Have students cite evidence in the discussion. Ask, "Why should we classify this animal in this group? This animal belongs in this group because _____ ."

YOU DO TOGETHER

1. Have student pairs continue to identify other criteria for classifying the photographs.

2. Have students provide evidence in each photograph that supports the lesson objective.

YOU DO ALONE

1. Have individual students produce their own design of animal classification.

2. Have students draw on the Activity Sheet and label the classifications.

3. Independent work may serve as an assessment to monitor student progress toward the objective.

Differentiation for English Learners

- Have students work collaboratively using oral language to describe their classification.

  "The animal is classified in this group because _____ ."

- Encourage drawing when students struggle with writing.

- Guide students to a science word wall to assist with oral language and writing.

Writing for Transfer

Classify This! is a platform for writing. Students can progress into paragraph writing, which reinforces topic sentences and the use of supporting details. Use this time to provide expansion by having students reflect on the activity. Sample questions may include the following:

- What did you learn?

- How might you change your project if you did it again?

- Which project inspired you?

Integrating Technology

Grades K–1

Working individually or with a partner, students can play the animal classification game on **www.sheppardsoftware.com**.

Grades 2–3

* Review and reinforce classification of rocks and their color, shape, and texture using **www.sheppardsoftware.com**.

* Classify This! can also be effective when projecting a hierarchical array on a smartboard. Visual support of the structure plays an important role for understanding.

Reflective Questions

1. How does looking at the image allow you to analyze size as it relates to classification?

2. How does close reading of images and determining classification support science content?

Appendixes and Resources

Appendix A

Appendix B

Appendix C

Name:_____ **Date:**_____

Directions: Using this picture, answer the questions.

What's going on in this picture?

What do you see that makes you say that?

What more can we find?

Name:_____ **Date:**_____

Directions: Answer the questions about the picture.

1. What's going on in this picture?

_____

_____

_____

_____ .

2. What do you see that makes you say that?

_____

_____

_____

_____ .

3. What more can we find?

_____

_____

_____

_____ .

Name:_____ Date:_____

Directions: Using this picture, answer the questions.

What's going on
in this picture?

What do you see
that makes you
say that?

What more can
we find?

Name:_____ **Date:**_____

Directions: Read the image to write about what you know and, then, what you learned.

STEP 1 🔍

Write about what's going on in this picture.

_____

_____

_____

_____

_____

_____

_____

STEP 2 💡

Use what you learned to write about this picture again. Remember to use evidence from the image.

_____

_____

_____

_____

_____

_____

_____

APPENDIX
A

Teacher Reproducible: Use these photographs to play Who Is It?

Who Is It? Social Studies 2–3

Teacher Reproducible: Use these photographs to play Community Workers Who Is It?

Name:_____ **Date:**_____

Directions: Fill in the blanks with words that describe Cinderella and what she is doing.

_____

_ _ _ _ _ _ _ _ _ _ _ _ _ _ _ _ _ _ _ _

What does Cinderella look like? _____

_____

_ _

_____ .

_____

_ _

What is Cinderella doing? _____

_____

_ _

_____ .

Name:_____ **Date:**_____

Directions: Answer the questions about the character on the cluster. Then, fill in the blanks.

What does the character look like?

_____

_____

_____

_____

_____

_____

_____

_____

_____

What is the character doing?

_____

_____

_____

_____

_____

_____

_____

_____

_____

I know the character is _____

_____

because _____ .

Name:_____ **Date:**_____

Directions: Fill in the chart with words and phrases that describe George Washington Carver.

Physical Characteristics

_____

_____

_____

_____

Behavioral Characteristics

_____

_____

_____

_____

Name:_____ Date:_____

Directions: Fill in the character cluster with words/phrases that describe the person being studied or main character. Then, write a caption.

Physical Characteristics	**Behavioral Characteristics**
_____	_____
_____	_____
_____	_____
_____	_____
_____	_____
_____	_____
_____	_____
_____	_____
_____	_____
_____	_____
_____	_____
_____	_____
_____	_____

Caption: _____

_____

_____

Name:_____ **Date:**_____

Directions: Look at the picture(s). What is the setting?
How do you know? Write your answers on the lines below.

? Best Guess

Evidence ✗

This picture takes place _____
_____
_____ .

Name:_____ **Date:**_____

Directions: What can you tell about the image? Write your inference in the column on the left and the evidence to support it in the right-hand column.

? Inference

_____
_____
_____
_____
_____
_____
_____
_____
_____
_____
_____
_____
_____
_____
_____
_____

Evidence

_____
_____
_____
_____
_____
_____
_____
_____
_____
_____
_____
_____
_____
_____
_____
_____

Name:_____ **Date:**_____

Directions: Count the number of items in each picture. Cross out the picture that does not have the same number of items as the others.

Name:_____ **Date:**_____

Directions: Count the number of items in each picture. Cross out the pictures that do not have the same number of items as the others.

Name:_____ Date:_____

Directions: Which paintings have quadrilaterals? Cross out the painting that does not show quadrilaterals.

Name:_____ **Date:**_____

Directions: Which paintings have quadrilaterals? Cross out the painting that does not show quadrilaterals.

Name:_____ **Date:**_____

Directions: Find triangles, squares, and rectangles.

1. Circle the triangles with yellow.
2. Circle the rectangles with blue.
3. Circle the squares with red.

Name:_____ **Date:**_____

Directions: Find triangles, squares, and rectangles.

1. Find at least 3 triangles and circle them with yellow.
2. Find at least 2 squares and circle them with red.
3. Find 1 rectangle and circle it with blue.

Name:_____ Date:_____

Directions: Find triangles, squares, and rectangles.

1. Outline the triangles with yellow.
2. Outline the rectangles with blue.
3. Outline the squares with red.

Name:_____ **Date:**_____

Directions: Find triangles, squares, and rectangles.

1. Find at least 3 triangles. Outline them with yellow.
2. Find at least 2 squares. Outline them with red.
3. Find 1 rectangle. Outline it with blue.

Name:_____ **Date:**_____

Directions: Read each sentence. Cut out the pictures, and glue the matching picture to each sentence.

	The **wind** helps this seed travel.
	People help this seed travel.
	The **bird** helps this seed travel.
	The **river** helps this seed travel.
	The **rain** helps this seed travel.

Name:_____ **Date:**_____

Directions: Paste the pictures with your sentences on top of the correct stepping-stone.

Stepping-Stones: Science 2-3

Name:_____ Date:_____

Directions: Cut out the pictures. ✂ Then, place them on the appropriate stepping-stone.

Name:_____ **Date:**_____

Directions: Paste the pictures on the correct stepping-stone.

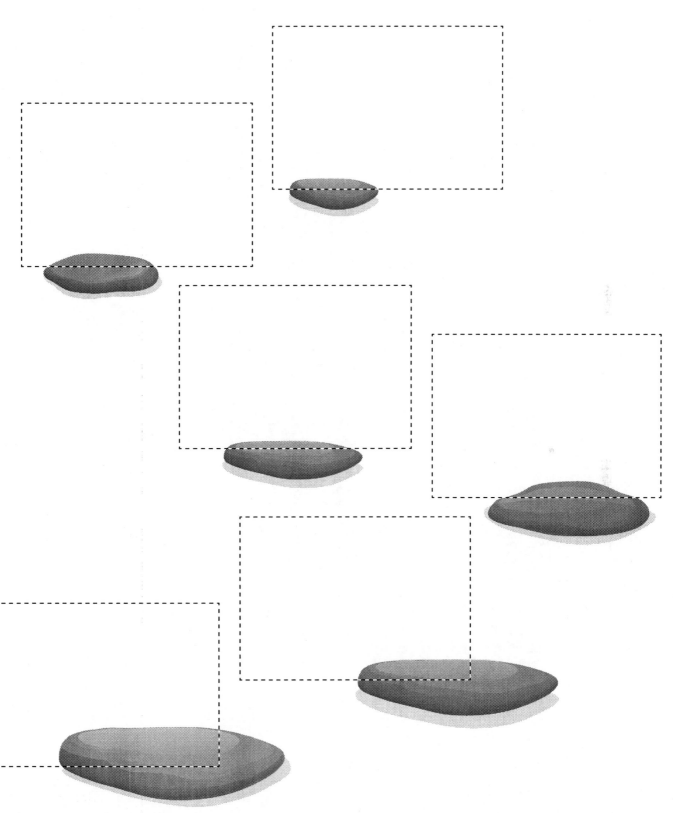

Name:_____ **Date:**_____

Directions: Using the pictures, make your best guess about the next topic we will be studying.

_____

The next topic we will study is _____ .

Name:_____ **Date:**_____

Directions: Using the pictures, list the common clues. Then, make a prediction about the next topic that will be studied.

Common Clues

I predict _____ .

Name:_____ **Date:**_____

Directions: Use the pictures to predict what the next science unit will be. Then, explain how you know.

The next topic we will study is _____.

Name:_____ **Date:**_____

Directions: Using the pictures, list the common clues and make a prediction about the next topic that will be studied. Then, explain your answer.

Common Clues

_____

_____

_____

_____

_____

_____

_____

I predict _____

_____

_____

_____

Name:_____ **Date:**_____

_____

- -

1. Close your eyes and think of _____ .

2. Open your eyes and draw what you saw.

3. Now that you have more information, draw a new picture.

4. Circle all the things in your second drawing that aren't in your first drawing.

Name:_____ **Date:**_____

1. Close your eyes and think of _____.
   Open your eyes and draw what you saw.

2. Now that you have more information, draw a new picture.

3. On the back of this sheet, write about the differences in your drawings.

Collaborative Text Information Maps: Social Studies **K-1**

Teacher Reproducible: Use these word, thought, and action bubbles to highlight text with students.

What is being said?

What is being thought?

What is being done?

Name:_____ **Date:**_____

Directions: Draw a map of where the text takes place. Then, place symbols, pictures, key events, or quotations where they belong on your map.

	1	2	3	4	5	6	7	8	
J									J
I									I
H									H
G									G
F									F
E									E
D									D
C									C
B									B
A									A
	1	2	3	4	5	6	7	8	

Name:_____ **Date:**_____

Directions: After reading or listening to the story, draw three key events in the order they happened.

Name:_____ **Date:**_____

Directions: After reading the text, draw six key events in the order they happened.

Name: _____

Date: _____

Directions: Using the pictures from the story, place each one where it belongs on the excitement graph.

	1	2	3	4	5	6

Name: _____

Date: _____

Directions: Using six pictures from the story, place each one where it belongs on the excitement graph.

	Event 1	Event 2	Event 3	Event 4	Event 5	Event 6
thrilling						
exciting						
engaging						
ordinary						
dull						
boring						

Name:_____ **Date:**_____

Directions: Draw the shapes named in the first column. Then, fill in the second column with its description.

Draw two shapes.	My **triangles** have:
	_____

	_____
	_____

Draw two shapes.	My **rectangles** have:
	_____

	_____
	_____

Draw two shapes.	My **squares** have:
	_____

	_____
	_____

Name:_____ **Date:**_____

Directions: Draw a shape from the anchor chart in the first column. Then, fill in the second column with its description.

Draw here.

_____

_____

_____

_____

_____

Draw here.

_____

_____

_____

_____

_____

Draw here.

_____

_____

_____

_____

_____

Name:_____ **Date:**_____

Directions: Draw a picture of a house in the space provided. Use the squares to measure how tall and wide your house is. Write the number of squares in the blanks provided.

_____ squares tall   _____ squares wide

Name:_____ **Date:**_____

Directions: Draw a picture of a bridge in the space provided. Use paper clips to measure how big your bridge is, and record the measurements on the picture.

Name:_____ **Date:**_____

Directions: Choose a picture. Glue it in the first box. List its properties. Then, glue a picture in the second box with the same properties.

		Properties

		Properties

		Properties

Name:_____ **Date:**_____

Directions: Create or find three images to place in the second column that have different properties (e.g., round, purple, hard). Write the property in the space provided. Then, glue two more images that belong in each category.

Properties	Image 1	Image 2	Image 3
Shape _____			
Color _____			
Texture _____			

Name:_____ **Date:**_____

Directions: Write the topic to be studied at the top. Then, glue or draw pictures that will form categories.

_____

- -

_____

Name:_____ **Date:**_____

Directions: Write the topic to be studied in the top box. Then, draw images that will form categories.

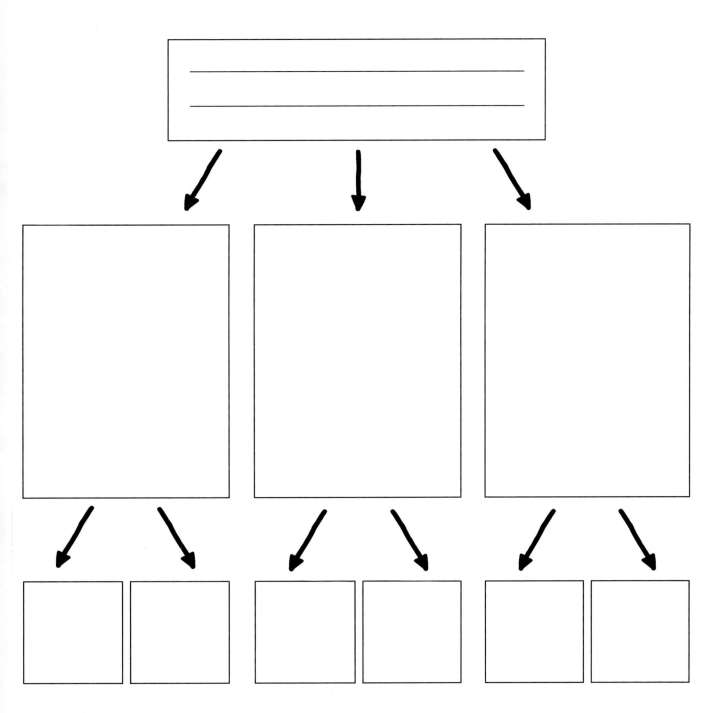

Digital Resources

Accessing the Digital Resources

The digital resources can be downloaded by following these steps:

1. Go to **www.tcmpub.com/digital.**

2. Enter the ISBN, which is located on the back cover of the book, into the appropriate field on the website.

3. Respond to the prompts using the book to view your account and available digital content.

4. Choose the digital resources you would like to download. You can download all the files at once, or you can download a specific group of files.

ISBN:
9781493880805

Please note: Some files provided for download have large file sizes. Download times for these larger files will vary based on your download speed.

 ## Contents of the Digital Resources

- Activity Sheets
- teacher reproducibles
- images for lessons
- Stepping-Stones alternative lesson cards (2–3)

Section 1

Albers, Peggy. 2001. "Literacy in the Arts." *Primary Voices K–6* 9 (4), 3–9.

———. 2006. "Imagining the Possibilities in Multimodal Curriculum Design." *English Education* 38 (2), 75–101.

Beck, Isabel L., Margaret G. McKeown, and Linda Kucan. 2002. *Bringing Words to Life: Robust Vocabulary Instruction.* New York: Guilford Press.

Britsch, Susan. 2009. "ESOL Educators and the Experience of Visual Literacy." *TESOL Quarterly* 43 (4): 710–721.

———. 2010. "Photo-Booklets for English Language Learning: Incorporating Visual Communication into Early Childhood Teacher Preparation." *Early Childhood Education Journal* 38 (3): 171–177.

Cappello, Marva, and Karen E. Lafferty. 2015. "The Roles of Photography for Developing Literacy across the Disciplines." *The Reading Teacher* 69 (3): 287–295.

Cappello, Marva, and Nancy Walker. 2016. "Visual Thinking Strategies: Teachers' Reflections on Closely Reading Complex Visual Texts within the Disciplines." *The Reading Teacher* 70 (3): 317–325.

Castek, Jill, and Richard Beach. 2013. "Using Apps to Support Disciplinary Literacy and Science Learning." *Journal of Adolescent & Adult Literacy* 56 (7): 554–564.

Cortazzi, Martin, and Lixian Jin. 2007. "Narrative Learning, EAL and Metacognitive Development." *Early Child Development and Care* 177 (6–7): 645–660.

Cozolino, Louis J. 2013. *The Social Neuroscience of Education: Optimizing Attachment and Learning in the Classroom.* New York: W. W. Norton.

Cummins, Sunday, and Ruth E. Quiroa. 2012. "Teaching for Writing Expository Responses to Narrative Texts." *The Reading Teacher* 65 (6): 381–386.

Eisner, Elliot W. 2002. "What Can Education Learn from the Arts about the Practice of Education?" *Journal of Curriculum and Supervision* 18, no. 1 (Fall): 4–16.

Essley, Roger. 2010. *Visual Tools for Differentiating Content Area Instruction.* New York: Scholastic.

Flavell, John H. 1977. *Cognitive Development.* Englewood Cliffs, NJ: Prentice-Hall.

Gambrell, Linda B., and Paula Brooks Jawitz. 1993. "Mental Imagery, Text Illustrations, and Children's Story Comprehension and Recall." *Reading Research Quarterly* 28 (3): 265–276.

Gangwer, Timothy. 2005. *Visual Impact, Visual Teaching: Using Images to Strengthen Learning.* Thousand Oaks, CA: Corwin.

Goodwin, A. Lin, Ee Ling Low, Pak Tee Ng, Alexander S. Yeung, and Li Cai. 2015. "Enhancing Playful Teachers' Perception of the Importance of ICT Use in the Classroom: The Role of Risk Taking as a Mediator." *The Australian Journal of Teacher Education* 40 (4): 131–149.

Heath, Shirley Brice, and Shelby Wolf. 2005. "Focus in Creative Learning: Drawing on Art for Language Development." *Literacy* 39 (1): 38–45.

Holloway, Susan M. 2012. "Visual Literacies and Multiliteracies: An Ecology Arts-Based Pedagogical Model." *Language and Literacy* 14 (3): 150–168.

International Reading Association and National Council of Teachers of English. 1996. *Standards for the English Language Arts.* Newark, DE: International Reading Association and National Council of Teachers of English.

Kandel, Eric. 2012. *The Age of Insight: The Quest to Understand the Unconsciousness in Art, Mind, and Brain, from Vienna 1900 to the Present*. New York: Random House.

Krashen, Stephen. 2008. "Language Education: Past, Present and Future." *RELC Journal* 39, no. 2 (August): 178–187.

Lee, Hyunju, and Allan Feldman. 2015. "Photographs and Classroom Response Systems in Middle School Astronomy Classes." *Journal of Science Education and Technology* 24 (4): 496–508.

Marzano, Robert J., Debra J. Pickering, and Jane E. Pollock. 2001. *Classroom Instruction That Works: Research-Based Strategies for Increasing Student Achievement*. Alexandria, VA: Association for Supervision and Curriculum Development.

Messaris, Paul. 1994. *Visual "Literacy": Image, Mind, & Reality*. Boulder, CO: Westview.

National Governors Association Center for Best Practices and Council of Chief State School Officers (NGACBP and CCSSO). 2010. *Common Core State Standards for English Language Arts and Literacy in History/Social Studies, Science, and Technical Subjects*. Washington, DC: National Governors Association Center for Best Practices and Council of Chief State School Officers.

Paquette, Kelli R., Susan E. Fello, and Mary Renck Jalongo. 2007. "The Talking Drawings Strategy: Using Primary Children's Illustrations and Oral Language to Improve Comprehension of Expository Text." *Early Childhood Education Journal* 35 (1): 65–73.

Ranker, Jason. 2014. "The Role of Semiotic Resource Complexes in Emergent Multimodal Reading Processes: Insights from a Young Student's Reading of a Comic Book." *The Australian Journal of Language and Literacy* 37 (3): 151–160.

Serafini, Frank. 2012. "Expanding the Four Resources Model: Reading Visual and Multi-Modal Texts." *Pedagogies: An International Journal* 7 (2): 150–164.

Sinatra, Richard. 1986. *Visual Literacy Connections to Thinking, Reading and Writing*. Springfield, IL: Charles C. Thomas Publishing

State Board of Education (SBOE). 2017. *Texas Essential Knowledge and Skills for Kindergarten–Grade 12: 19 TAC Chapter 110: English Language Arts and Reading, Subchapter A*. Austin, TX: Texas Education Agency.

Vygotsky, L. S. 1978. *Mind in Society: The Development of Higher Psychological Processes*. Edited by Michael Cole, Vera John-Steiner, Sylvia Scribner, and Ellen Souberman. Cambridge, MA: Harvard University Press.

Wilhelm, Jeffrey D. 1997. *"You Gotta BE the Book."* New York: Teachers College Press.

Wood, J. Luke, and Frank Harris III. 2016. *Teaching Boys and Young Men of Color: A Guidebook*. San Diego, CA: Center for Organizational Responsibility and Advancement.

Zygouris-Coe, Vicky I. 2015. *Teaching Discipline-Specific Literacies in Grades 6–12: Preparing Students for College, Career, and Workforce Demands*. New York: Routledge.

Section 2

Cappello, Marva. 2017. "Considering Visual Text Complexity: A Guide for Teachers." *The Reading Teacher* 70 (6): 733–739.

California State Board of Education (CSBE). 2000. *History-Social Science Content Standards for California Public Schools, Kindergarten Through Grade Twelve*. Sacramento, CA: California Department of Education.

Conklin, Wendy. 2004. *Applying Differentiation Strategies: Teacher's Handbook for Grades K–2.* 2nd ed. Huntington Beach, CA: Shell Publishing.

Fisher, Douglas, and Nancy Frey. 2014. "Addressing CCSS Anchor Standard 10: Text Complexity." *Language Arts* 91 (4): 236–250.

Fisher, Douglas, Nancy Frey, and Diane K. Lapp. 2016. *Text Complexity: Stretching Readers with Texts and Tasks.* Thousand Oaks, CA: Corwin.

Kress, Gunther, and Theo van Leeuwen. 2006. *Reading Images: The Grammar of Visual Design.* 2nd ed. New York: Routledge.

National Governors Association Center for Best Practices and Council of Chief State School Officers (NGACBP and CCSSO). 2010. *Common Core State Standards for English Language Arts and Literacy in History/Social Studies, Science, and Technical Subjects.* Washington, DC: National Governors Association Center for Best Practices and Council of Chief State School Officers.

Sierschynski, Jarek, Belinda Louie, and Bronwyn Pughe. 2014. "Complexity in Picture Books." *Reading Teacher* 68 (4): 287–295.

Wood, J. Luke, and Frank Harris III. 2016. *Teaching Boys and Young Men of Color: A Guidebook.* San Diego, CA: Center for Organizational Responsibility and Advancement.

Yenawine, Philip. 2003. "Jump Starting Visual Literacy." *Art Education* 56 (1): 6–12.

———. 2013. *Visual Thinking Strategies: Using Art to Deepen Learning across School Disciplines.* Cambridge, MA: Harvard Education Press.

Section 3

Blachowicz, Camille, and Peter J. Fisher. 2010. *Teaching Vocabulary in All Classrooms.* 4th ed. Boston: Pearson.

Cappello, Marva, and Nancy Walker. 2016. "Visual Thinking Strategies: Teachers' Reflections on Closely Reading Complex Visual Texts within the Disciplines." *The Reading Teacher* 70 (3): 317–325.

Housen, Abigail. 2007. "Art Viewing and Aesthetic Development: Designing for the Viewer." In *From Periphery to Center: Art Museum Education in the 21st Century,* edited by Pat Villeneuve, 172–179. N.p.: National Art Education Association.

McKeown, Regina G., and James L. Gentilucci. 2007. "Think-Aloud Strategy: Meta-Cognitive Development and Monitoring Comprehension in the Middle School Second-Language Classroom." *Journal of Adolescent & Adult Literacy* 51 (2): 136–147.

Vogt, MaryEllen, and Jana Echevarría. 2008. *99 Ideas and Activities for Teaching Learners with the SIOP Model.* Boston: Pearson.

Yenawine, Philip. 2013. *Visual Thinking Strategies: Using Art to Deepen Learning across School Disciplines.* Cambridge, MA: Harvard Education Press.

Yenawine, Philip, and Alexa Miller. 2014. "Visual Thinking, Images, and Learning in College." *About Campus* 19 (4): 2–8.

Zygouris-Coe, Vicky I. 2015. *Teaching Discipline-Specific Literacies in Grades 6–12: Preparing Students for College, Career, and Workforce Demands.* New York: Routledge.

References Cited

Children's Literature Cited

Dillon, Patrick. 2014. *The Story of Buildings.* Massachusetts: Candlewick Press.

Hoban, Tana. 2000. *Cubes, Cones, Cylinders, & Spheres.* New York: Greenwillow Books.

Nouvion, Judith. 2015. *Shapes.* New York: Houghton Mifflin Harcourt.

Rice, Dona Herweck. 2015. TIME For Kids. *Good Work: Plant Life.* Huntington Beach, CA: Teacher Created Materials.

Tonatiuh, Duncan. 2010. *Dear Primo: A Letter to My Cousin.* New York: Abrams Books for Young Readers.

Section 4

Allen, Janet. 2014. *Tools for Teaching Academic Vocabulary.* Portsmouth, NH: Stenhouse.

Brooks, Margaret. 2009. "Drawing, Visualisation and Young Children's Exploration of 'Big Ideas.'" *International Journal of Science Education* 31 (3): 319–41.

Coleman, Julianne M., Erin M. McTigue, and Laura B. Smolkin. 2011. "Elementary Teachers' Use of Graphical Representations in Science Teaching." *Journal of Science Teacher Education* 22 (7): 613–643.

Hayik, Rawia. 2011. "Critical Visual Analysis of Multicultural Sketches." *English Teaching: Practice and Critique* 10 (1): 95–118.

Herrell, Adrienne L. 1999. *Fifty Strategies for Teaching English Language Learners.* Upper Saddle River, NJ: Prentice Hall.

McConnell, Suzanne. 1992. "Talking Drawings: A Strategy for Assisting Learners." *Journal of Reading* 36 (4): 260–269.

Nagy, William E. 1988. *Vocabulary Instruction and Reading Comprehension: Technical Report No. 431.* Champaign: University of Illinois at Urbana-Champaign.

Paquette, Kelli R., Susan E. Fello, and Mary Renck Jalongo. 2007. "The Talking Drawings Strategy: Using Primary Children's Illustrations and Oral Language to Improve Comprehension of Expository Text." *Early Childhood Education Journal* 35 (1): 65–73.

Whitin, Phyllis. 2005. "The Interplay of Text, Talk, and Visual Representation in Expanding Literary Interpretation." *Research in the Teaching of English* 39 (4): 365–397.

Zoss, Michelle, Richard Siegesmund, and Sherelle Jones Patisaul. 2010. "Seeing, Writing, and Drawing the Intangible: Teaching with Multiple Literacies." In *Literacies, the Arts, and Multimodality*, edited by Peggy Albers and Jennifer Sanders, 136–156. Urbana, IL: National Council of Teachers of English.

Children's Literature Cited

Adler, David A. 1999. *How Tall, How Short, How Faraway.* New York: Holiday House.

Aliki. 1988. *A Weed Is a Flower: The Life of George Washington Carver.* New York: Aladdin Books.

Aliki. 1999. *My Visit to the Zoo.* New York: HarperCollins.

Davis, Cathy Mackey. 2006. *Postal Workers Then and Now: My Community Then and Now.* Huntington Beach, CA: Teacher Created Materials.

De la Peña, Matt. 2015. *Last Stop on Market Street.* New York: G. P. Putnam's Sons Books for Young Readers.

Gibbons, Gail. 2009. *Coral Reefs.* New York: Holiday House.

Herweck, Diana. 2011. *A Day in the Life of a Firefighter* (TIME for Kids Nonfiction Readers). Huntington Beach, CA: Teacher Created Materials.

Hoberman, Mary Ann. 2007. *A House Is a House for Me.* New York: Puffin Books.

Holub, Joan. 2005. *Who Was Johnny Appleseed?* New York: Penguin Group.

James, Helen Foster, and Virginia Shin-Mui Loh. 2013. *Paper Son: Lee's Journey to America.* Ann Arbor, MI: Sleeping Bear Press.

Jovin, Michelle. 2017. *Fantastic Kids: George Washington Carver* (Time for Kids Nonfiction Readers). Huntington Beach, CA: Teacher Created Materials.

Kroll, Jennifer. 2010. *George Washington Carver: Planting Ideas.* Huntington Beach, CA: Teacher Created Materials.

Kuntz, Doug, and Amy Shrodes. 2017. *Lost and Found Cat: The True Story of Kunkush's Incredible Journey.* New York: Crown Books for Young Readers.

Schwartz, David M. 2003. *Millions to Measure.* New York: HarperCollins Children's Books.

Settle, Melissa A. 2006. *Firefighters Then and Now: My Community Then and Now.* Huntington Beach, CA: Teacher Created Materials.

Steptoe, Javaka. 2016. *Radiant Child: The Story of Young Artist Jean-Michel Basquiat.* New York: Little, Brown Books for Young Readers.

Wallner, John. 1987. *City Mouse-Country Mouse and Two More Mouse Tales from Aesop.* New York: Scholastic.

Yolen, Jane. 2011. *Johnny Appleseed: The Legend and the Truth.* New York: HarperCollins.

Notes